EMPOWERMENT

through

WITCHCRAFT

© Desiree Groom

About the Author

Dr. Linda Murphy is a Third-Degree Wiccan, a high priestess, and an elder in the Craft. She has a PhD in Geography. Visit her online at www.MagickOfTheWeek.com.

A Wiccan Guide
for the Magickal Practitioner

EMPOWERMENT
—— *through* ——
WITCHCRAFT

LINDA MURPHY, PhD

LLEWELLYN PUBLICATIONS | WOODBURY, MINNESOTA

FIRST EDITION
First Printing, 2023

Book design by R. Brasington
Cover design by Shannon McKuhen
Editing by Marjorie Otto
Interior art by Llewellyn Art Department: 14, 45, 176

Photography is used for illustrative purposes only. The persons depicted may not
    endorse or represent the book's subject.

Llewellyn Publications is a registered trademark of Llewellyn Worldwide Ltd.

Library of Congress Cataloging-in-Publication Data (Pending)
ISBN: 978-0-7387-7449-7

Llewellyn Publications
A Division of Llewellyn Worldwide Ltd.
2143 Wooddale Drive
Woodbury, MN 55125-2989
www.llewellyn.com

Printed in the United States of America

For my nephews who, along with their children,
have kept me ever mindful of the need to educate the future.
And to their mother, my sister Myra,
for letting me be "other mother."

Acknowledgments

As always no one writes a book without a tremendous amount of assistance along the way. *Empowerment Through Witchcraft: A Wiccan Guide for the Magickal Practitioner* is no different. It is a long list and I hope I don't leave anyone out.

First, I have to acknowledge my former partner because he was there oh so long ago when this book first began. When after many years I pulled out the original copy, his editing notes were still there. They were good then, and I used them.

I also have to acknowledge my nephew, Nathaniel. He was the one who said that it was time I wrote a "how-to" book for witchcraft. He was right. Aside from that he has always been assistive with his techno-magick, including getting my music back up and running.

My friend Cynthia did early reading and editing. She identified the "more" that *Empowerment Through Witchcraft: A Wiccan Guide for the Magickal Practitioner* needed. She also had some valuable input about using illustrations. Along with her, my friend Nancy did some early reading and editing and as always, her input was invaluable.

During the writing of *Empowerment Through Witchcraft: A Wiccan Guide for the Magickal Practitioner* I started practicing the use of herbs again. It is Wicca 101 to learn and know your herbs and I had strayed from that knowledge. My friend Lynda reminded me that I was ignoring ages old wisdom long practiced by the Wise Women and Wise Men. She introduced me to a whole new set of friends, herbalists, who shared their immense amount of lore with me. Two specifically, Karen and Jimmy, became the best of friends. I owe these people a huge thank you.

Obviously, I have had the honor of knowing many witches, shamans, and magick practitioners along the way. No matter how they interacted with me, good, bad, or indifferent, they had a tremendous influence on how I evolved as an empowered witch, and I am grateful to each and every one.

Jade's presence in my life has been a non-stop reminder that we can never just stop and rest on our laurels. We must ever strive to be better than we were yesterday.

I cannot ignore the invaluable contribution of my editor, Heather Greene. She said yes to this book. Second, her editing work, along with that of Marjorie Otto, made it a much stronger book.

May *Empowerment Through Witchcraft: A Wiccan Guide for the Magickal Practitioner* be a reminder to all that when faith is practiced with intent to grow and evolve, then it can yield immeasurable power.

Blessed be.

CONTENTS

Exercises

FOREWORD

Dr. Linda Murphy and I go back thirty years in this incarnation and have been friends in several other incarnations as well. It is an honor and a pleasure for me to write this foreword to her book *Empowerment Through Witchcraft: A Wiccan Guide for the Magickal Practitioner.*

She has forgotten more about witchcraft than most witches ever learn. Her deep wisdom and understanding of the magickal power available to Wiccans are invaluable in providing solid ground upon which to build personal empowerment and new levels of inner growth and spiritual understanding. Her expertise in working with powerful energies, both simple and complex, is stunning. I attribute this to her remarkable development of both her right brain and left brain. Her analytical gifts are matched by her intuitive gifts and she's a master of both modalities.

There is an experiential nature to magickal practices that makes them very powerful. They impact both our conscious and unconscious minds in a lasting way that promote inner growth and outer mastery of energies that are active in our lives.

Dr. Murphy's many years of being a university professor have enabled her to develop an acute sense of what is engaging to listeners and readers and what will help them enjoy and retain the information she provides in a clear and polished way. This book gives Dr. Murphy the perfect platform to express her myriad talents and dazzle readers with her breadth of knowledge, depth of insight, and light a path for those on the path of personal growth and spiritual evolution to follow and enjoy.

Cynthia Katharine Lee, MA
Founder and administrator of the Mystical Order
of the White Rose

INTRODUCTION

You are a witch. Perhaps you have chosen Wicca as your religious expression of your faith and you can cast a circle. You celebrate the seasonal turns of the Wheel of the Year. The power of the lunar cycle is something you use regularly. You create spells and know that those spells will work. You have reached a point in your magickal life that has led you to look for something that will evolve your soul to its next step. You are ready to use the tools of Wicca for self-empowerment.

I am also a witch and for a long time Wicca has been my personal religious choice. My practice includes many different forms including Gardnerian Wicca, Ceremonial Magick, and folk practices. What I have discovered from the gnosis of these many forms is that while the tradition matters to a person's religious needs, spiritual evolution can be reached in any religious system. This is the difference between faith and religion. Religion is an organized system of values and practices. Faith occurs when you believe in something without evidence or proof. Our religious choice reflects how we wish to express our faith.

Those religions, or paths of any form, tend to be consistent and teach the same basic lessons: a teacher is a teacher; a healer is a healer; a hunter is a hunter; a warrior is a warrior. Yet to reach the fullness of expression in any one religion, the tools of that specific form must be used to their greatest extent. Doing so will allow a person to search deep inside themselves to become completely aware of their spiritual power, accept responsibility for that power, and, eventually, begin to express that power in a state of enlightened self-interest. If one is following the true will of one's higher self, which is enlightenment to achieve self-empowerment, then one will have a positive effect on the world. This is the fullest expression of faith through one's religious path.

As I evolved through my own journey, I began to take on students who were seeking to learn magick. Most of my students were Wiccan, but some were not. With all the forms available to them, my goal was to teach them how to use Wiccan tools within any religious form to continue their personal evolution. I believe that one of the great strengths of Wicca and witchcraft is that these are highly flexible belief systems that can be adapted to meet the needs of the practitioner. Beyond teaching the basics of Wicca, I also taught my students how to use the tools of Wicca to reach self-empowerment.

Wicca has, at its core, some great tools that can be used to achieve a fullness of personal power. As an earth-based religion, Wicca teaches that the use of natural energies around us—such as that from the earth, sun, moon, stars, and planets—can affect our internal growth. Those energies are always around us; they always exist. Our celebrations of the seasonal sabbats and lunar esbats do not create this energy, rather, it is already there and we are attaching to it through our rituals and spellwork. With the conscious knowledge that we are attaching to what is already there, we can use the flow around us to empower ourselves. We need never fear that there is a finite amount of that energy, either. The energy available to us is as limitless as the cosmos itself. This teaching is one of the gifts of modern Wicca: how to use that limitless cosmic energy to develop our own self-empowerment.

Ultimately, my own practice of Wicca and witchcraft are unique to me and, as you proceed along your path, I encourage you to make Wicca and witchcraft unique to yourself.

A Brief History of Modern Wicca

Modern Wicca is the gnosis of many occult and spiritual teachings and yet maintains an individual presence in its use of the tools of nature to celebrate the soul. Some Wiccans have, in the past, attempted to trace a long religious history back to Neolithic humans and beyond to back up their current religious practices. It is a strong need in many people to legitimize their religious choice by citing unbroken history and tradition and using that history to give their beliefs a lineage, even if it's not completely accurate.

The truth is modern Wicca, as it is mostly practiced today, is a child of the twentieth century. The simple version of the story is that a man named Gerald Gardner claimed to have been initiated in rural England into the New Forest Coven in 1939. This group practiced the folk magick of English witchcraft and was led by a woman named Dorothy Clutterbuck. Gardner incorporated the rites of Ceremonial Magick into his version of witchcraft because of his relationship with Aleister Crowley, a leading member of the Ordo Templi Orientis (OTO). Gardner and Crowley met in 1947 and Gardner was initiated into the Ordo Templi Orientis by Crowley. Gardner then studied under Crowley. In 1950, after Crowley's death, Gardner wrote a letter in which he talked about Crowley's interest in folk magick traditions. Gardner stated in the letter that

Crowley had encouraged him to continue working with the New Forest Coven, practicing traditional folk magicks and incorporating the rites of the OTO into the practices of the Coven.[1] We do not know how much of what Gardner stated, from the existence of Dorothy Clutterbuck and the New Forest Coven to his statements about Crowley encouraging him to combine the two traditions, is true. However, what we do know is that over the next fourteen years Gardner combined the very formal tenets of Ordo Templi Orientis with what appeared to be folk magick traditions of rural England, along with his own beliefs about the God and Goddess into a practice. In doing this he created the basics of modern Wicca.

Gardner's student Raymond Buckland brought modern Wicca to the United States in 1963, and, through the 1960s, Gardnerian witchcraft was the established baseline for Wiccans. During that time, the women's movement in the United States began to incorporate Gardnerian witchcraft into their consciousness-raising efforts. In California, the Compost Coven was born, opening the door to what is more commonly practiced a half-century later.

Two books emerged from the Compost Coven that would have tremendous impact on the evolution of modern Wicca. Margot Adler wrote *Drawing Down the Moon*, published in 1979, an academic work that looks at the practices of modern witches. Also, in 1979 Starhawk published *The Spiral Dance*, a book of rites and practices that incorporated both the history of Gardnerian Wicca and tenets from the women's movement. Those two books brought modern Wicca out of the shadows and introduced it to the public, making Wicca as a religion more accessible to the public.

---

1. Ronald Hutton, *The Triumph of the Moon* (New York: Oxford University Press, 2005), 205, 297.

Is there an unbroken line of Wiccan religion to prehistoric humans? Are there secret covens that have never lost their Book of Shadows over the centuries? Did ancient ancestors stand and call the four quarters to create sacred space? Most likely not. Ultimately, shamanism is the oldest known form of religious or spiritual practice, with practices dating back over 30,000 years. The oldest records are out of Siberia, but hunter/gatherer groups from Asia, Tibet, North and South America, central Europe, and Africa also practiced forms of shamanism.[2] What little we know about the practices of these folks, magick included, comes from what these groups left behind: rock and cave drawings and paintings, pottery art, and relics in grave sites. For thousands of years magick and the mundane world were not considered separate things. Shamans and other wise women and men were also the leaders, doctors, and warriors of their communities.

About 6,500 years ago, the advent of cities in the region of the Tigris and Euphrates rivers and the Fertile Crescent gave rise to hierarchical state level societies. Those cities were dominantly theocracies, ruled by the priestly class. This began the separation of the mundane and the magickal.[3] The rise of Christianity and Islam led to the persecution of older religions. Although the pre-Christian ways were shunned, many people continued to practice the old ways—even if it was hidden—through folk medicines and folklore. Those traditions were handed down through the generations, continuing the traditions locally through celebrations and rituals.

---

2. Bonnie Aronson, "History of Shamanism," accessed September 12, 2022, http://firstlightemp.com/history-of-shamanism.html.

3. Les Rowntree, Martin Lewis, Marie Price, and William Wyckoff, *Diversity Amid Globalization: World Regions, Environments, Development* (Upper Saddle River, NJ, Pearson Prentice Hall, 2009), 297.

Wicca, as it is practiced today, is the result of centuries of religious evolution, as are all other modern religions. Are there family traditions that are still practicing Wicca from centuries before? No, but many folk magicks have been handed down from one generation to the next within almost all religious forms, including Christianity. My own grandmother would be scandalized if I told her that washing the greens under running water three times—and always and only three times—was a form of folk magick, but that is what she learned from her grandmother, taught her own daughter, and, ultimately, what I learned.

Wicca as a Mystery Religion

Since those early days, Wicca has become more and more commodified, and, as that has happened, it has drawn in more and more people who have no desire to train for priestess or priest roles. Many of these people simply want to celebrate and take part in a religious form that worships both God and Goddess. This current trend in Wicca is a positive step and has led to gaining constitutional protection of our religious rights as well as a more accepting attitude from the larger society. However, there is a tendency to forget that Wicca is also a mystery religion. As a mystery religion, it is a faith-based belief system that focuses on the self-empowerment of the individual.

One of the great mysteries is that each person is their own priest or priestess. That sounds so simple, yet it is also very hard to understand. This understanding must be reached in steps. Those steps are the initiatory rites that some modern Wiccans choose to walk. Each stage of these rites is connected to a person's deeper understanding of what their personal power is and how to use it. A dedicant knows the same things that a third degree knows. The difference is the level of knowledge of what to do with that information and the internal connections that were made in reaching their own power.

Another one of the great mysteries is this simple statement: "I believe that I can, therefore I can." We all know that statement to be true. The difference is how well we are able to live that statement; how many self-deceptions block our internal power so that they do not really believe from deep down inside that they can, or that they are responsible for the outcome if they do. One of the greatest blocks is the need to blame someone else for the results of one's actions. The more personal responsibility you take, the more you are able to do what you believe, or wish, that you can. As you evolve through the Wiccan mysteries, you learn how to stop the self-deceptions, stop being afraid of the responsibility, and reach the higher levels of believing that you can.

You become self-empowered. You become your own priest or priestess.

Here is another great mystery: you are the center of your own circle, your own reality, and your own matrix. From that center, it is often difficult to read the entire matrix without the assistance of others. It is often not possible to determine how you and your energy are affecting all the variable threads that are flowing from you into your personal reality. Growth and accepting your power and the responsibility for that power allows you to see more and more of how you create the reality—the circle—around you in both a positive and a negative way.

Once you accept responsibility for your power, you can no longer pretend to be a victim of circumstances or the will of others. You are the priest or priestess in a circle of your own creation, good or bad. Taking personal responsibility is, of course, a frightening step, and many people choose not to take it because they do not want to accept that all of their reality is created by them. They no longer have someone else to blame when things go wrong. However, you are empowering yourself every time you accept responsibility for your creation and, as a result, you become increasingly able to create the reality you want. Using the tools of Wicca can help seize that power and put it in your hands.

Power in Your Hands

As Wiccans, we grow through contact with natural forces. We consciously attach to those forces with seasonal rituals and spell-work. By doing no more than attaching our fortune to the Wheel of the Year, we are guaranteed more awareness of who we are and how we affect our personal reality. Learning and living, the basic tenets of the Wiccan Rede and the Law of Three, can give a witch a sense of personal responsibility and insight into their own motivations for their actions. The Wiccan Rede points out that we should "harm none." The Law of Three states that whatever energy you put out there will come back to you. Of course, we may not always like what we see or what needs to be changed. Wicca assists there, too. By following the Wheel and the movements of deities through their annual trials, we can discover ways to change ourselves internally so that our external reality becomes what we want. We begin to truly believe that we can, so we do.

My Personal Story

I grew up in the netherworld between the Baptists and the Catholics of the Deep South. I was raised Baptist, but in my twenties converted to Catholicism. During my teens, I studied various magickal paths intermittently, at least what was available at that time. One night, I did a spell and went to bed. During that night I had a visitation, and not of the gentle sort. I woke up in terror and burned what few books I had. I did not practice any magick at all for the next decade. However, college opened new ways to view the world and introduced me to a whole new set of people. Some of those people were serious practitioners in various magickal traditions. I spent a lot of time with many of them and I explored those practices, which led to a crisis of faith in my religion. During that period, a dear friend gave me a copy of Starhawk's *The Spiral Dance*. Finally, I had found my true path, and, in the summer of 1983, I began a serious study of Wicca. That year was basically my year and a day as a dedicant. During Litha in 1984, I took my first degree with two ceremonial mages attending as witnesses. I have never looked back.

For the next twelve years, I practiced as a solitaire or with very small groups. Believe me, during that time period if you could find someone with whom to work, it was nothing short of a miracle. I did have a group of friends who were all mages of some sort or another. One of them was a Ceremonial Magickian, who taught me the basic tools of Ceremonial Magick that I still use today. I do believe that it was my interactions with him that turned me into a teacher who respects and encourages cross-training in magickal paths.

As I worked through my second degree, I faced and fought a lot of inner darkness. I also attained two academic master's degrees. By Samhain 1995, I was ready to begin my third degree work, but I was not in a place where there was a teacher or a group with which to work. However, the tides of life were changing.

I began my doctoral work in 1992. It was part and parcel of the work I was doing in my third degree. Near Ostara 1996, I met a man who was already practicing Wicca. His enthusiasm lit the fuse. We held a semi-public rite during Lughnasad 1996. Before I knew what was happening, I was standing as the High Priestess of a large Wiccan circle. I also became a teacher and acquired a new teacher of my own, who was a shaman and one of the finest energy workers I have ever known. Using energy movement as his medium, he taught people how to become aware of their own personal power and how to effectively use that power in a positive way. My work deepened my understanding of myself and made me a much stronger teacher.

I finished my doctorate. That enthusiastic Wiccan I had started public rites with was now a third degree, a high priest, and my partner. Together, we started teaching Wiccan classes at a local venue, which led to a whole new circle, a teaching circle. Our students grew and began taking on students of their own. All of us used these venues to spread the word that our religion can, and does, have a positive effect in a person's spiritual evolution.

Ask me what kind of Wicca I practice and it's a long answer. I am very eclectic. I was trained in the traditional degree system of modern Wicca, very Gardnerian. My own personal practice is dominantly Irish Faery Wicca with heavy doses of Ceremonial and shamanistic magicks.

Underlying those things is my own ethnic and cultural background. My family heritage is both Irish and Native American of the Chickasaw and Choctaw tribes. I am deeply steeped in folk practices that have come down to me from all of these rich traditions, which have flavored the Deep South of the United States. Although I have formal training, I am a witch who practices the folk traditions that have come to me from ancestors who knew that the world was full of magick.

Wicca Brings Change

This book is not another "how to cast a circle or spell" guide. Wicca can and should be used to affect internal changes within a witch. Its tools and how they are used for self-empowerment is the focus of this book and is open to everyone.

Traditionally, modern Wiccan practice has been dependent on a gender binary in its worship of the God and the Goddess. That is how I, and many others, learned the practice. But gender roles and definitions are changing, expanding, and redefining in our world today. What a wonderful time to reach for self-empowerment using witchcraft. Finding new definitions of self and living true to those definitions is a part of self-empowerment. The path is open to all.

The basic lessons of Wicca are augmented with true stories of people who have shared the magick of Wicca with me. It is my strongest hope that this book will give words of growth to all of those who would walk a magickal path. No matter what religious tradition you choose to follow or how you identify, you can empower yourself by using the tools of witchcraft and Wicca, and this book helps teach you the ways to do that.

Chapter One

WHEEL OF THE YEAR

One of the first things you probably learned when you started practicing witchcraft or the Wiccan tradition was the Wheel of the Year, the magickal calendar that many witches follow as part of the ongoing evolution of the earth and of themselves. It is a series of sabbats or celebrations that allow the faithful to rejoice in the cycle of life around them and celebrate the God and the Goddess in all their aspects. This eight-spoked Wheel is also a tool that can be used for personal growth. As you pass each spoke of the Wheel, you can take advantage of the place you are in time to make real and significant changes in your own life. It is a helpful tool for perfecting the spell that is you because you are connecting to the seasonal energy and the deity within yourself.

The Wheel begins with Samhain, the witch's new year, and continues with each sabbat. The four astronomically-based seasonal celebrations are Yule, Ostara, Litha, and Mabon. These celebrations come primarily from Norse traditions. The cross-sabbats are Samhain, Imbolc, Beltaine, and Lughnasad. These four agriculturally-derived sabbats came into Wicca mostly from the Celtic traditions. By combining these astronomical and agricultural markers, we have a calendar that celebrates all the motions of the earth and the sun throughout the year and the seasonal changes we see around us.

Using the Wheel of the Year as a tool for self-empowerment, you can mark your new calendar with the eight major sabbats to enhance your spiritual journey with the power of each sabbat. Check out all the astronomical movements, including lunar phases, of the coming year so you can use them most effectively for your personal spells. Buy an almanac and a new date book. You will make your plans in spring so that your dream can come to fruition in autumn.

Here is quick refresher of each sabbat, in case you are not following the Wheel now, and a way to use each one to promote your personal growth and self-empowerment.

Figure 1: Wheel of the Year

Samhain

During Samhain, the veil between the worlds of the living and the deceased is thin, as thin as it will be throughout the year. You may have heard this mentioned before, but what does that mean? Samhain is the time of the year when the final harvest takes place and the God becomes a gateway to other realities, opening doorways for us to view the probabilities that surround us. The Goddess opens the door and we walk through. The dark is overcoming the light. The Crone is in her strength. She wields the power to reach the Dark Lord in the Otherworld and make the door open so that we can look through. This is a time for remembering, dreaming, and foretelling.

Scrying

Samhain is the new year in Celtic traditions. One of the ways we prepare for the new year is to scry. There are a multitude of ways to do this, and most are useful, if used properly. While you can scry any time of the year, if you are doing it as part of a Samhain celebration, do your scrying before or during a Samhain rite. Invite your ancestors or your former selves to talk to you and impart the wisdom that they have gained from the Death Lands about your personal growth and the things you need to work on.

Scrying is a call to all the spirits. If you open yourself to their voices, they will provide the wisdom you need for the coming year. Hearing the advice from spirits can be a lot harder than it sounds. We all have such a powerful image of what we want from life that sometimes that image overshadows what we actually need to be working on. Your ancestors and other spirits can provide a very different perspective. This is a critical moment in developing your personal strength. The ability to listen and follow their advice, even if it is unpleasant, puts the power in your hands to create the best possible future for yourself.

How do you make sure you are open to what those voices are telling you? You may have celebrated a lot of Samhain rites, some as a solitaire and some with other Wiccans or witches. The peak of the Samhain rite is most commonly at midnight on the 31 of October as it becomes November 1, also known as All Saints' Day. This is the time to formally call to the spirits to speak to you. However, a whole lot of preparation and activity takes place before this moment, before the circle is cast and the rite begins. You can use each preparatory step along the way to make yourself more receptive to what you will hear when the voices start talking to you during the formal rite. You might even scry before the ritual begins to simply send an invitation out to spirits.

As a witch, you may already know multitudes of ways to scry. Pick the method you feel most confident in using. Whenever you do your scrying, in ritual or out, remember two things: first, you are officially inviting all those spirits, particularly ancestors, to come and speak to you. Second, you need quiet so you can concentrate and be open to those spirits.

You can also use the secular Halloween festivities to make yourself more open to the lessons you are getting from beyond. If you are participating in trick-or-treating by joining the little ones in any way, then you are putting out a very joyous welcome mat for those spirits. Many of your ancestors will join you because they love the sound of children laughing. They are not coming to cause harm. They are there to relish the living legacy of their bloodline. The trickster energies are out and about as well, so make sure the innocents are magickally and physically protected. Then join in the fun, keeping in mind that you are consciously welcoming the loving spirits into the fun as well.

Once the little ones go to bed, the adult part of Samhain begins. The night sky will fill with all types of spirits, some friendly, some not so friendly. If you are preparing to go into a formal Samhain rite, use the energies already circling around. Cast a formal circle to keep you protected from imbalanced energies. You have opened the door to the spirits and made them welcome; do not be afraid to accept the words of even the more threatening ones. If a scary spirit makes it through your circle, then it is balanced. All those spirits may be whispering to you about what you need to accomplish in the coming year. Loving spirits will be gentle in their words. However, it is often the darker spirits who tell us what we really need to hear. Listen to them all. When the conversations are over, send all of them on their way before you open your circle. Be sure to thank them when you say goodbye.

You are lucky beyond belief if you get an immediate, clear verbal response to your questions. More commonly, you will receive images and feelings that take time to interpret. These answers become clear over a period of days, often in your dreams. Sometimes it takes all the way until the next sabbat, Yule, for complete clarity. Do not get impatient. You opened yourself to those voices. They spoke to you. Let the wisdom they shared evolve into your consciousness as you are ready to accept it.

Samhain night becomes All Saints' Day on November 1. If possible, go to a cemetery where some of your ancestors are buried. If that is not possible, take time at home to remember those loved ones who have passed. They still love you and have given you valuable advice. This is a perfect time to let them know that you heard their voices and you are ready to manifest their lessons in your quest for self-empowerment.

In the midst of all the fun of Halloween, celebrate the final harvest and cuddle up with a cup of chocolate, cider, or tea in front of a fire. Dream the dream that is you at your best and what you will have to do to get closer to that best.

 Exercise
Samhain Scrying Ritual

There are multitudes of ways to scry. One of my favorites is using a mirror. Any mirror will do. I call on my ancestors for advice about the coming year. I am blessed to have a huge mirror that was my grandmother's, which is the one I normally use for scrying.

You will need: a mirror.

Once you have your mirror, find a quiet place. This is a time for you to have a conversation with those to whom you call. You do not need any disturbances from this side of the veil to interrupt the conversation. Create a safe and sacred space. Quiet yourself, breath slowly, and let go of your daily life.

Once you are calm, gaze into your mirror and call out to whom you wish to speak. You can call them by name or in a more general way. For example, I make a general call to my ancestors and to my former selves. Quietly wait to see who shows up. Your own reflection in the mirror may well begin to shift as other images emerge.

The mirror works well in presenting not only images of those you have called, but also images of what the coming year holds for you. Those images are sent from the spirit realm. You listen by keeping the images in your memory. The images will assist you in shaping your spells for the rest of the year.

When the images cease and only your reflection remains, take a deep, cleansing breath. Say thank you to those who answered you call. Open your sacred space. Go enjoy the rest of Samhain.

Yule, the Winter Solstice

The winter solstice arrives six weeks after Samhain. It is the longest night of the year. The seasonal sabbats are all based on the relationship of the earth to the sun. There are subtle changes in that relationship from year to year, which is why the solstices and equinoxes shift the date on which they occur from year to year. The winter solstice occurs when one of the earth's poles has its maximum tilt away from the sun. The winter solstice is the day with the shortest period of daylight and longest night of the year. In the Northern Hemisphere that event happens sometime between December 20 to December 22 or sometime between June 20 and June 22 in the Southern Hemisphere.

The wisdom from the spirits that was imparted to you at Samhain should now be clear to you. This is a time to begin to feel sure of what you want to change in your life and to be reborn in order to birth that change into reality. This is harder than it sounds. Some dreams want to remain dreams and you must be willing to coax them out into the open. Yule is the sabbat during which we give names to our goals so we can start the journey in the coming year.

Yule Vigil

In my own tradition, we begin the Yule celebration with a night-long vigil. This vigil coaxes what was a vague idea into reality by giving it a name. At Samhain you set forth on a quest to listen to the advice of the spirits about what you should plan. Their loving voices imparted the knowledge of what you needed, inspiring you to reach deeper into your power. The harsher voices may have named the fears and doubts that you must face in order to achieve your goals. A formal Yule vigil addresses both types of messages, serving two very important purposes. First, it allows the doubts and fears to rise and be examined. These are the moments that truly test your faith in yourself and your dreams. You must feel those doubts and fears and have your faith tested in order to truly celebrate when the sun rises.

The second reason for the vigil is to deeply examine all the dreams and what you will plan for the year. The vigil gives you a long, quiet period to really examine all that you have absorbed. During this time of stillness, you have the space to reach deep inside and finally, truly define your plan so you can celebrate its birth with the sunrise. In order to claim your dream and start working toward it, you have to conquer the fear inside of you that will try to block that dream and keep it from becoming a reality.

Ideally, at dusk, as the sun sets on the longest night of the year, you close and lock the doors and begin the vigil. Of course, our modern world does not always allow for that to happen. Dinner has to be served; children must be fed, bathed, tucked in; nightly household chores have to be done. Most likely you will have to go to work the next day and also get some sleep yourself. Even if that is your reality, try and set aside some time to sit in your own sacred space and do an attenuated vigil.

Reflect on everything that you heard at Samhain as it becomes clearer in your mind. What name does your dream go by or your plan take? What doubts and fears will you face in achieving that goal? Be sure to be up at sunrise and watch that happen. Celebrate yourself and your goals. This courage will assist you throughout the year and help develop your power year after year.

While you are beginning this journey, do not forget that this is also a time of great rejoicing and celebration. Remember the Christmas celebrations of your youth? Recapture that feeling and have fun. Give gifts to those you love and do it with a joyous heart. Open your own gifts with the abandon of a child. Eat too many sweets. Spend time with loved ones reminiscing, telling stories, and just enjoying their company. Birth your new dream. Then, nurture it so it can grow.

After all that celebrating comes what is often called the post-holiday letdown. January is a time of quiet and nurturing. Much like a mother nurtures her newborn baby, now you can hold your newly named dream close and give it some attention in your heart and mind. What needs to be done to accomplish this dream this year? What will stand in your way and how best to avoid those blocks? At what points on the calendar do you intend to take definite steps toward realizing this dream? Use the energy of quiet rest and get ready for the next spoke in your journey of self-empowerment.

Exercise
Yule Vigil Meditation

This may be a year when you cannot spend all night in a vigil. Maybe you only have one or two hours before sleep takes over your consciousness. You can use that time to do an attenuated vigil using this meditation.

You will need: a piece of paper, a pen or pencil.

Go to your sacred space. Calm your mind and heart. Once you have reached that quiet inside yourself, call up the words or images you've had inside you since Samhain. Let those ideas become real things in your mind. Give them names. If there are scary ideas, those are fears. Name those fears. Giving anything a name, wish or fear, gives you power over it. If possible, write down all the things you have named.

Once you've named these ideas and written them down, open your sacred space. Put the paper where you have written down the ideas on your altar. Go get some sleep.

Imbolc

Imbolc has a tendency to sneak up on us. This is the mid-point of winter and is usually celebrated on or around February 2. Wiccans love to perform their rites outdoors, if possible, but Imbolc is the one that is often celebrated indoors. Obviously, that is partly because the weather is often not too comfortable for outdoor rites. Another reason is that Imbolc is a celebration of hearth and home. If you can celebrate it inside next to a fireplace, then do so.

This year's journey is taking its next big step. You are challenged to reach for your personal identity and find the deity within you. It is a big moment for your year and for your overall sense of self-empowerment. You are expanding your self-definition, embracing the divine within you. Your identity gets bigger because of your own choices as well as the way society sees you. It is all too easy to lose yourself in all the definitions you have acquired. Only you have the right to determine how you self-define. Personal empowerment ultimately occurs when you make that decision on your own and you do not let yourself be defined by your relationships with others.

Imbolc is the time to cast your dream (the one you clarified at Yule) to the cosmos so the cosmos can work on the future for a while. Take the physical part of the spell, amulet, talisman, writing on paper, whatever you created at Yule to represent the spell, and go out at some point during Imbolc and focus on the spell. Ask the cosmos to take care of it for a while for you. That leaves you to focus on the moment and your definition of self. Seek yourself and what makes you powerful while the cosmos is working on your goals. Now is the time to remember who you are when you are at your best and free from all the definitions that are placed on you. Remember who you really are and always wanted to be.

You begin this part of the Wheel's journey excited about the new adventures calling to you, but a little nervous about leaving old ways and definitions behind. The Fool card of the tarot explains it beautifully. In most decks, the figure of the fool is about to step into the future, but is also glancing over their shoulder at their past.

Do not forget to honor your home during Imbolc; it is the place that has gotten you this far and it will be the place to which you will return. Yet, at the same time, the ground is getting ready for planting just as your soul is getting ready for your dream to be planted inside it. This is not the dream others have for you, but the one that is yours and yours alone. Remember how to stand as an individual and seek some adventures to remind you of your strength.

Exercise
Meet Myself

It is time to let the cosmos take care of your wishes and fears for a while.

You will need: the paper from Yule, a clean piece of paper, a pen or pencil, a mirror.

Sit with the paper of named things that you wrote at Yule. Read each one, out loud if possible. If it's a fear, let yourself feel that fear. Visualize the wishes coming true. Take all the time you need. When you are done, burn that piece of paper! For now, forget it. Ask the cosmos to take care of it for a few weeks.

Now, go through your self-definitions. Start with the definitions society has placed on you. Add the ones you give yourself, positive and negative. Write them down if you wish. Get your mirror and see yourself in all those roles. At the end ask yourself, "Who am I in all those definitions?" Gaze into the mirror until you see the you that you wish to be. Say hello to that you and accept that is who you are at your core. All the other definitions begin with this definition.

Looking into the mirror, start to see yourself as the definition you like the most. When that image is complete, say hello to your true self.

Open your space. Go out into the world using the only definition that matters, the one that makes you feel confidant and joyous.

Ostara, the Vernal or Spring Equinox

The two equinoxes, spring and fall, are the two moments in the year when the sun is exactly above the equator and day and night are of equal length at the equator. The vernal equinox, which marks the beginning of spring in the Northern Hemisphere, can occur any time between March 19 to the 21. In my tradition we call this day Ostara.

The ritual of Ostara is one where sexual innocence and curiosity are the order of the day. It is a time of flirting, dancing, and courting. This is a time to call upon your memories or your dreams of first love and the promise of love consummated. Sexual innocence is about the dream of love and what you want to be. Ostara is about the joy of life and the ritual should reflect that. Music, picnics, eggs, flowers, and candy can be incorporated into the ritual itself.

For adults, the innocence of Ostara can be difficult to find inside themselves. This is a good sabbat for working on your self-empowerment, as well as other annual goals, by exploring your own sexual or gender identities. If your sexual identity has caused you emotional damage because you didn't fit society's definitions of what you should be, this is a rite where you can take back your power. Reach for the moment inside yourself when you were innocent and had not yet been hurt. Let that innocence fill you now so that what is right for you can grow without pain. Give yourself permission to be true to who you are. Allow that definition to be without pain. Acknowledge yourself as an individual and know how powerful you are when you stand alone. Empower yourself without judgment, your own or anyone else's.

Put on some soft-colored spring clothes, dye some eggs, pick a daisy, dance with the fairies, and celebrate. You should be feeling the first stirrings of the changes inside of you as your fears start to be resolved and your strength begins to emerge from the depths into the sunlight. The spring equinox is here, and the cosmos has sent back the first promise of a future harvest. With the softest of early spring breezes, the gentle rain, and the sun and the moon hanging equally in the sky, Ostara is the promise of tomorrow.

 Exercise
Reclaiming Your Innocence

At Imbolc you saw your core self in the mirror, who you are without definitions. That is you at your most innocent before anybody's definitions, including your own, began to shape you. Ostara is the sabbat when you can reclaim that innocence.

You will need: just yourself.

Go outside on Ostara. Feel the sun, maybe a soft breeze. Pull that sweet, innocent image of you into your head. See that person growing and evolving into the person you wish to become. Do not try to go past the image. That comes later. For now, simply start from that innocent foundation to define who you want to be.

Finding your innocence before you took the blows life sent you is not easy at all, but the energy at Ostara will help and provide the space for you to try.

Beltaine

The promise of spring is a promise no more. The season is now in full bloom. The fields are fertile and plowed and ready to accept the seeds that will guarantee life's continuance. The flirtation between earth and sky is a flirtation no more. Consummation and conception take place. The plants know it, the animals know it, and the people know it. This is the mid-point of spring. I have always celebrated it from sundown on April 30 through sundown on May 1.

Beltaine is traditionally made up of fertility rites and is very sexual. This is the energy that gets all the other energies moving so that creation can take place. Creation of new life requires sexual contact, but creation of any kind can get a boost of sexual energy at Beltaine. In its highest form, Beltaine is the sabbat that gives you the creative energy to begin to manifest your dreams each year and your overall sense of empowerment. You can use the sexual energy of Beltaine to bolster your work, whether you are a solitary witch or in a group. If in a group, you must start with this statement: all sexual acts must be consensual.

Consensual sex between adults can be very empowering. However, the important part to remember is that the sexual energy has to be creative, healing, and loving. Sexual energy works, in whatever fashion you generate it, because it is the energy that sparks all the other energies into action. Sexual energy is the beginning of creation and when it is moved, through ritual and magick, into other creative areas then the possibilities for growth become greater. Take sexual energy from the rite, or your activities after the rite, and use it to enhance your projects, your dreams, your goals and also encourage your inner power to grow. Again, remember that, if you are performing a sex rite with someone else, their dreams and self-empowerment are important, too. It is very satisfying to share energy with others, whether you share physically or spiritually, and be part of their dreams. Alone or with others, you can use the creative energy of this sabbat to take the innocence of Ostara and turn it into the self you wish to become. Then, spread the blessing of Beltaine in whatever way you choose.

Exercise
Beltaine Visualization

Your greatest self-actualization comes when you recognize that you have gifts that others need, and you share those gifts. This exercise will help.

You will need: your mirror.

At some point during this sabbat go into your sacred space. Take a mirror with you. Sit for minute and reach your calm center. Leave the mirror reflective side down for now. Visualize all the life force around you. Plants and animals are growing. See them in your mind's eye.

Now visualize the creative force inside your own body. Access the power of that force and let it spread throughout your whole essence.

Pick up that mirror. See yourself as you let your own creative energy fill you. Let the image that is looking back at you become the person you want to be. Your own creative power can combine with the creative power of Beltaine to propel you into growth.

When you are comfortable with the image of what you are becoming, put the mirror away. Open the space. Go smell some flowers and enjoy spring in its fullness.

Litha, the Summer Solstice

Summer's heat is just beginning to make itself felt at this time, but it has not gotten as hot as it will get. The longest day of the year has come. It is Litha, the summer solstice. In the Northern Hemisphere the solstice occurs anywhere between June 20 through June 22, depending on how the Earth and the calendar are aligned with the sun. There are other names for the summer solstice. Most commonly you will see it called Midsummer.

Using the Wheel of the Year to promote your own spiritual growth, realize annual goals, and develop your own empowerment now takes a new direction. As the plants in the fields begin to grow, so do the weeds that would choke out their lives and bring the harvest to an early end. Your fears may begin to be felt really strongly now. Fears can be sneaky and laziness is one of the ways that fear can hide: "I'll do it tomorrow, there will be time." Your growth needs attention now. It can't wait for tomorrow. Commit to the idea that work is required, and if it was easy, anyone could do it. These are your dreams and your power. Prove that you are willing to work to achieve those goals.

Litha rites are usually dominated by the power of the sun at its greatest strength. Often there is a moment when the darkness reveals that it is always there, waiting to take the power of light away. As you go into your rite, consider that struggle as a metaphor for the struggle inside yourself. Now is the time to make a deep commitment to your goals for the year. Yet, the darkness within you may be holding you back from that commitment. Your Litha rite, whether with a group or as a solitaire, can make that its focus.

As winter has January to rest, summer has July. The crops are on their way and aside from weeding and making sure they get enough water, there is not much else to do. However, instead of a time of quiet contemplation, this is a time of great activity. Time to nurture that growing dream inside yourself, give it all the attention it needs. Empower yourself by promoting who you are. Be like the sun in its great summer power. Shine brightly as yourself and allow nothing or no one to silence your voice. Feel your power growing inside you. If you encounter resistance from others or outright hostility, then defend your right to be the person you choose to be.

Enjoy some summer fun. Spend some time traveling, visit with friends, shop, work the fields, or weed your patio garden. Get a tan or a sunburn, celebrate life in all its aspects, and feel the power of the sun at this time, for Lughnasa is not too far away. The first harvest is about to begin.

 Exercise
Become the Monarch of Your Reality

This is the perfect day to draw on the power of the sun to reveal and dispel the fears and doubts that are standing between you and your goals. Nothing can hide under the light of the sun at Litha.

You will need: your mirror, sunscreen.

Take some time to soak that power into yourself. As close to solar noon as possible, take your mirror and cast a circle, outside if possible. Look into the mirror and see your fears and doubts. When you have seen as many as possible, turn the reflective surface of the mirror to the sun. Ask the sun to dispel those fears and doubts. Do not be surprised if the mirror shatters as the sun's power does its job. This will not bring bad luck but instead open you to letting yourself grow past the negatives that have held you back.

Once that part is done, call the light and heat of the sun into yourself. Feel your whole essence fill up with your strengths. Let yourself believe that you have everything you need to become the monarch of your own reality.

Stay in that sunshine for as long as you can, but before you get sunburned, open your circle. Be sure to clean up any broken glass if necessary. Take the power of you that the sun has shown you into some summertime activity. Believe that you rule your reality.

Lughnasa

As the temperatures rise, the sun is actually burning the life away from the fields. Lughnasa has arrived. It is the midpoint of summer and is traditionally celebrated August 1 through August 2. The three harvest festivals—Lughnasa, Mabon, and Samhain—are celebrated in a variety of ways. Most typically, it is taught that during this time of year, the God gives up his life and crosses over to the Death Lands to learn the secrets of other worlds to bring back those secrets at Yule. You will see this sacrifice and crossing represented in rituals in many different ways and at different sabbats. All are fine as long as you get the chance to feel the sacrifice, the mourning, and the crossing over. I have always celebrated the death of the God at the first harvest of Lughnasa. This ritual has the double aspect of gratitude for what is given and the preparation of what will be granted in the next harvest because of willing sacrifice. Lughnasa is a reminder that in this world, life feeds on life.

Now is the time to look for the seeds that you planted at Beltaine and have since grown. Are projects coming to fruition? Are you feeling the fruits of your goals becoming your reality? It is a time to witness the beginning of their return to you as the first harvest. While that happens, you must also joyfully sacrifice something that continues to hold you back. It cannot be something that is easy. A sacrifice is just that, a sacrifice. Dig into your power and remind yourself that if it was easy, anyone could do it. As painful as it can be to give up a bad habit or something else you love, you will find the space to do so with love and joy. This can even be some lie you tell yourself about who you are—good, bad, or indifferent—that might be standing in the way of your dreams. Now is the time to name that lie and sacrifice it so that it no longer stands in your way. Trust that anything you sacrifice will be returned to you as energy—better and greater than what it was.

In the weeks between Lughnasa and Mabon, you should be able to see the rewards of a year of hard work. Your dream is now in full harvest. Your life should be blessed with all the things that you once only dreamed would come about if you reached for personal growth. Prepare for the great harvest because the final moment of this year's dream is about to reveal itself.

 Exercise
Lughnasa Casting Off Rite

It would seem simple, but the hardest part of preparing for Lughnasad is deciding what sacrifice you are going to make. We all have negatives in our reality that are holding us back. We all know we need to sacrifice those negatives in order to grow in our personal power. Yet, we are often deeply attached to the very things that are holding us back.

You will need: only yourself.

Over the past year you have put a lot of energy into defining your fears and doubts. Now it is time to let go of at least one of those things, but you may be hesitant about making the choice. Take some time before this rite to figure out why you are so deeply attached to the negatives that are holding you back.

Go into your sacred space. In your mind, look at each negative you believe to be true about you. Ask yourself why you chose to believe that negative. Really listen to what your heart tells you about each one and what it says about yourself for believing each one. Choose one of those negatives to sacrifice at the rite.

Keep reminding yourself that if it was easy, anyone could do it.

Mabon, the Autumnal Equinox

Mabon is the name that we give to the autumnal equinox. Once again, the sun is exactly above the equator and day and night are of equal length. The Northern Hemisphere experiences Mabon sometime between September 20 through September 23 as the sun crosses the celestial equator going south. This is the great harvest, the time of greatest rejoicing that all the work of the year has come to fruition. It is also a time to mourn for what you sacrificed to achieve that harvest.

Mabon is a time to let go of the past and to no longer be bound by its power; to let go of the projects that did not bear fruit and aspects of yourself no longer needed. This is an essential part of your annual journey on the Wheel of the Year, but also of your spiritual growth. The person that you once were should be mourned before the new person can truly take power. This is one of the things that can be accomplished at a Mabon ritual. Take time to review the past year.

If you are a solitaire, set aside some private time for this work. If you are in a group, you can make mourning part of the ritual. Either way, speak of what you gave up at Lughnasa so you could make room for a more empowered you. Tell the story of the year's journey. If tears come, let them fall. Do not be ashamed of true sorrow about any failings or what you had to sacrifice. Once you have mourned and are fully ready, embrace the new you and where you are at that moment. If it helps, look into a mirror and see who you were and who you are now.

Now celebrate the great harvest. Have a piece of apple pie or cup of cider or both. Light a fire. Let joy fill you as you acknowledge your own power, your own self-definition. If you are celebrating with others, then congratulate them for their work. If you are alone, do not be shy about congratulating yourself for the work you have done to reach this point. Thoroughly enjoy this moment because Samhain is only six weeks away. A whole new year will begin and you'll be able to aim for a new goal and continue growing your power.

Exercise
Mourning Meditation

You have worked so hard to grow and evolve in your own power. You cannot wait to celebrate the new you. However, deep inside you know you will miss some aspects of the old you. That is what the mourning aspect of Mabon embraces.

You will need: only yourself.

Spend a few minutes before the rite to embrace the old you. That person is leaving, never to return. It is time to say goodbye. Get into your sacred space. Once you are calm in your center, go through the memories, happy and sad, of living as that person. Cry. Let yourself truly mourn what you have released. As negative as it may have been, it was part of your self-definition. There was something about that definition that you loved. That is why you held on to it for as long as you did. It is perfectly okay to mourn for what you are no more.

Once you're finished, go celebrate who you are now.

A Yearlong Spell

The use of spellcasting, along with the power inherent in the ever-turning Wheel of the Year, allows each sabbat to bring you closer to your immediate goals and the bigger goal of taking back your personal power. This type of spell is a yearlong commitment because it works directly with the eight sabbats. Each spoke adds another layer to the spell's accomplishment of its goal.

Taking advantage of the naturally flowing energies, this spell opens doors to the abundance of gifts around us and allows those gifts to enter your life. Setting up a Wheel of the Year spell adds your will to each spoke. Following are two spells that I and others have used. You can tweak each spell to match your instincts and tradition. Just be sure to stay consistent and focus the energy of the spell at each sabbat.

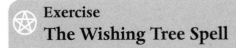

Exercise
The Wishing Tree Spell

This spell is designed to use each spoke of the Wheel to do two things: First and obviously, to add the energy of the Wheel to making your wishes come true. However, on a deeper level, watch as, at each spoke, your understanding of why you wished for those things evolves.

You will need: eight strips of paper, a pen, a glue stick, and a tree branch.

During the night of the Yule vigil, take a few minutes to take eight strips of paper and write a wish on each one. Each wish must be a different wish; you cannot duplicate wishes. Put the papers with your wishes aside until daylight. At sunrise, randomly draw one wish and take your glue stick and make that strip into a circle. Then put the wish on a tree. Any tree will do as long as it is special to you and you can access it for the whole year.

As the Wheel turns, at Imbolc, take one of your wish strips and add it to the first, looping them together. This is beginning of a ribbon of wishes. Going forward, at each sabbat, continue the ribbon, randomly drawing a wish strip, and adding it to the ribbon.

At the next Yule you will not add a new wish but complete the ribbon by making it into a circle on the tree. Now let the forces of nature take your wishes away. Don't fret if the ribbon has already become tattered throughout the year. It just means that the cosmos is paying attention to your spell.

Exercise
Abundance Spell

It is a rare person who does not want more abundance, usually financial abundance, in their lives. As the spokes of the Wheel turn and you add coins, watch how your definitions of abundance evolve.

You will need: a piggy bank, eight coins.

Get a piggy bank and at Yule put a coin in it. Then at every following sabbat add a coin to the bank. Any type of coin will do; do not add bills and do not spend the coins or look at them until next Yule. Then, at the following Yule, remove all the coins and go spend them on whatever you want or give them away. Either choice is fine as long as you get the coins out into the cosmos so that you are sharing yourself and your power. You can do whatever your instincts say to do with the piggy bank itself; keep it, give it away, or destroy it.

When to Start a Yearlong Spell

Traditionally, the old year ends at Samhain, October 31. The new year begins then as well. However, I believe that the period between Samhain and Yule is a period of rest and meditation on what has passed and what is about to come. As the sun rises on Yule morning, a new reality begins. That is why I start my Wheel of the Year spells on that sabbat. They set in motion a building of the new reality. However, the Wheel is a circle, so you can start anywhere. Below is a brief explanation of each sabbat so you can decide what works best for you in using the spells above or putting together your own Wheel of the Year spells.

Yule—Starting the spell with the nightlong vigil, in some form, offers the perfect time to meditate on intentions and start the spell off strongly. Then you can bless the spell with the power of the rising sun on Yule morning.

Imbolc—If you choose to start your spell here, then you are starting it by casting it to the cosmos. The cosmos will work on the spell now and you are free to pursue other things for the next few weeks. The ground is getting ready for planting and your soul is getting ready for the spell to be planted inside it.

Ostara—Choosing to start the spell here reflects the idea of life renewed, life eternal. It is a time of beginnings. You are starting the spell with the energy of innocence and all that is new.

Beltaine—You can start the spell here with all the force and creativity of a farmer fertilizing future crops or of animals and humans fertilizing the future so new creatures can be born. Effectively, you are starting your spell with that type of energy.

Litha—This sabbat is a great time to start the spell with a sense of commitment to seeing it through all the way around the Wheel. It will make a statement that your power is something you believe in and that your spell will work.

Lughnasa—If you start your spell here, you must go into the first casting of it with a sense that you are willing to make sacrifices over the course of the year to reap rewards. You must also trust that anything that you sacrifice will be returned to you.

Mabon—Starting your spell at this sabbat means that you begin this cycle with great rejoicing and a touch of sadness. You mourn for what you have given up for this spell and rejoice at what you have.

Samhain—It is always good to start a new spell with a dream of what you want the coming year to hold. The spirits will guide you to what needs to be changed for you to become more self-empowered.

Wherever you start any spell, especially those to develop your power, celebrate each spoke on the Wheel, never forgetting that it is a circle, and you will always return to where you began. The only difference will be that you will have evolved, grown, and expanded, if you have been faithful in performing the spell on each sabbat.

Chapter Two
DRAWING DOWN ENERGY

While the sabbats are seasonal holidays, the esbats are generally smaller rites that include a formal circle cast and a working of some type. Like the Wheel of the Year, the esbats are also excellent tools to use for self-empowerment. Each cosmic body, such as the moon or a planet, has its own specific energy that you can draw down or call upon to work on a particular area that needs some attention. You may already be comfortable with doing spellwork with many of these energies. Usually, those spells aim the energy outward to affect the reality around you. It is time to aim that energy inward.

All types of drawing downs listed in this chapter were inspired by the rituals associated with drawing down of the full moon. That esbat is the most basic in any witch's handbook. Most witches start with that energy work and it's certainly the esbat ritual that has gotten the most press. However, there are many other energies in the cosmos. A discerning witch can be working on a Wheel of the Year spell and add any of these esbat energies if the need arises. It is a beautiful way to empower yourself.

What Is Drawing Down?

Before looking at the specifics of lunar, solar, and other types of drawing downs, it seems appropriate to provide a few general notes. In these rites you are pulling down the specific energy of a cosmic entity in order to use it to affect change in yourself, someone else (with their permission), or the world in general. The goal, as with any energy work, is to create a doorway to allow the energy into yourself. If you are performing the rite alone, then all that is necessary is to feel the energy, focus it on your goal, and then let it go. If the rite is with a group, then you become the doorway through which the others access the energy.

How do you decide what energy is correct for any given purpose? You choose by listening to your heart and meditating on your needs. That will lead you to the correct cosmic entity and particular aspect that will be most assistive. Sometimes you will plan an esbat in advance and invite other people to join you, making it an event. Sometimes you feel a need spur-of-the-moment and just do a drawing down, either alone or with other folks. Listen to the cosmos and take advantage of what it has in abundance. A key to figuring out the energies of any cosmic body is to stop and learn about each one; what its habits are and how it manifests in our sky. The key to understanding anything is very often observation, with all of your senses open and functioning.

One thing to remember is that you have always naturally used the energy around you—even that from the cosmos. The only thing that has changed since becoming a witch is your awareness of what you are doing. That awareness gives you precision in how to effectively use the energies to your best advantage and how to avoid offending or angering any misused energies. Nothing like having a planetary energy pissed at you!

Exercise
Drawing Down Energies

Regardless of what type of drawing down you are doing or with which energies you intend to work with, the basics of the rite are consistent.

You will need: items that correspond to the chosen energy; candles and incense are the place to start. After that you can use as many things as you wish, including dressing in the appropriate color.

Once you have decided on the work at hand and assembled the items that correspond to that energy, you can begin.

Always start by casting a formal circle. Then call the energy you wish to work with. If the work at hand is an honoring of cosmic energy, which is often the case with the moon, call the moon. Once you are certain that it has joined you, let your love for that energy fill the circle. Enjoy the relationship for as long as both you and the energy desire. Once it is over, thank the energy and release it. Be sure you ground yourself. Open your circle and take that glow with you as you move back to your normal reality.

When you are calling the energies to do specific spellworkings, the steps are the same, to a point. Once the energy is present, you will invest your spell with the power of that energy.

The only exception to this standard set of rules is when you do something spontaneously because the joy of the moment simply took over. Even then, be sure to thank the energy for its presence.

Whether working alone or with others, be sure to leave a space clear of the power of the entity. That is the responsible thing to do for others who will pass that way later.

The Moon

It would be very easy to fall into a poetic rhapsody about the moon, and certainly many have. Witches have a long-standing relationship with the Lady of the Night. In most Wiccan traditions the moon represents the Goddess, ever changing, never dying, being recreated again and again. There are some traditions, however, that view the moon as masculine.

Each night, and indeed each hour, the moon's phase changes a little. On the whole, however, there are four moon phases: dark, waxing, waning, and full. Within that context, the possibilities are endless as to precisely which energy you want to draw down in order to facilitate your workings, including personal empowerment. First, you can set up a month-long working that uses each phase in its way to promote a specific part of the working. Second, you can also use any particular moment of the lunar cycle to add a boost of energy to your efforts. You may have already done both of these with other types of spells. It works the same way for spells that put your own empowerment as their focus.

What follows is a brief guide to the energies of each phase and some helpful hints as to what you can do with each to strengthen your inner self. Beyond that, be creative. Look to the moon and get your inspiration in Her ever-changing face.

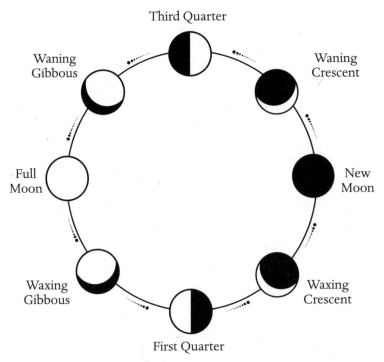

Figure 2: Moon Phase Diagram

Dark Moon

The dark moon, or new moon, is called the Crone's Moon because there is no moon. The Crone knows when to be silent and keep her magick to herself. She often shrouds her power in darkness. Her magick is not always dark magick, but it sometimes works best because it is hidden. A night with absolutely no moon in the sky occurs only once in the lunar cycle. If you want to use this energy, then plan carefully or you will miss it. Any other night there is at least a sliver of the moon. This phase's energy is probably the most dangerous, therefore any working requires extreme precision in order to get the results you want. There is not much room for error. This energy is neither kind nor understanding. In other words, the dark moon does not suffer a fool gladly.

The dark moon is a good place to start a spell if you want to begin removing something inside of you that is holding you back. An aspect of the dark moon is dreaming and prophesy and cleansing yourself of old ways of thinking in order to have a new start. The dark moon is the aspect of the moon most closely associated with death, both figurative and literal. The dark moon takes anything into death and prepares it for a rebirth into something new and transformed.

If you are doing a spellworking using a full lunar cycle, begin the working here with the death of the old way and a rebirth of the new pattern. If you have already seen what is blocking your empowerment, use this phase's energy to rid yourself of that block and to start a transformation in your life. This is also a good moon to use to identify those blocks inside yourself. Scry under the moon to assist you in that identification.

Waxing Moon

The moon begins to wax, or grow, immediately after the new moon or dark moon. With the first sliver in the sky, you are in the moon phase that is rich with possibilities for increase. The moon waxes larger each night over the next two weeks. This aspect is ready for change and, indeed, goes out and seeks change of any sort. Look inward for changes that are happening within you. This is a great time to more clearly define something about yourself that you wish could be growing in its influence. If you are doing full cycle lunar spellwork, early in this waxing moon phase is the time to state clearly what you want to happen as the moon approaches fullness.

Love spells and money spells are two that are going to be most popular during this moon phase. However, every witch, sooner or later, makes the mistake of casting one of those spells without really thinking it through. Money comes in, but you are working your butt off and cannot get enough time to go out and spend it. You have all the attention in the world from that special someone, or at least he or she was special until you could not get them to leave you alone. These may seem like amusing outcomes, but there can be outcomes that are not in the least amusing.

Remember, take care and ask for what you *need* not what you *want*. There is a difference. In fact, your own personal power increases when recognizing that difference. In many cases, what we need is not more money or love, but rather to be more loving or more generous or more aware of the flow of energy around us. One simple way to empower yourself is to ask for just those things to increase in your life and watch the magick happen.

Full Moon

Here it is: the full moon. Technically there is a limited amount of time for the exact full moon, but if you are doing spellwork, you have about three days before and three days after to get your act together. Of course, your best bet is the actual night of the Full Moon, and the closer to the hour of fulling, the better. If you are doing a working that is using the lunar cycle to empower yourself, this is when you should start feeling the effects. You should be stronger inside yourself and not fearful of letting your true self be seen.

I stated earlier that the dark moon was the most dangerous, and that is true, but the full moon in practice can also be very dangerous, mainly because it is so hypnotic that it lures you in and can make you do silly things. If you read tarot cards you already know that the full moon is the card of deception. Think of it this way, the full moon sheds light on the ground below, but it is dim light. That light may not reveal the things on the ground that might trip you and make you fall.

There are quite a few people who think this is the most powerful aspect of the moon. It isn't; it is just the brightest. This phase is when your full lunar cycle spellwork is showing results and that is one reason it is often considered the most powerful aspect. You have been working hard for two and a half weeks on your goal and now fruition is here. It doesn't happen at once when the moon is full, but over time.

Before I offend any witches or the Lady herself, I must add that the full moon has some very special traits that can be used. This is the Mother's Moon. Got something you want nurtured? Now is the time. This is also the place to go when you need a bit of reassurance that life is working out. The full moon is also a time when you can show your appreciation for all the cosmos has done for you, and it's a time of joy. Show your gratitude and celebrate the miracle that is your life. Revel in the energy that is before you and give thanks for what you have received while also asking for the blessings to continue.

Technically the full moon is when the spellwork is complete, but the lunar cycle is not so the work is not either. Use this phase's energy to recharge your batteries and prepare for the next phase. If you are doing a self-empowerment working and not feeling any more empowered than when you started, you should reassess the working. Take a minute and examine the original spell to see if it was not quite what it should be. The time for fixing things is about to begin.

Waning Moon

The Mother fades as the Crone begins to take the ascent again. This is the waning moon phase. It is its own unique phase that often goes unnoticed and uncelebrated, but it has specific energies attached to it that can be used quite effectively. Over the next two weeks as the moon gets smaller you can empower yourself greatly by harnessing this aspect in order to be honest with yourself about your work. What did you forget? What did you leave out?

This phase is the phase of banishing. You can get just about anything to go away by using the waning moon energies. Start your work about three days after the full moon and ask for the negative influence to have a diminishing power in your life. As the moon gets smaller, so will the influence, especially during the last quarter. This is a great time, for example, to get rid of bad habits, bad relationships, bad spells; you name it.

Waning moon energy to often used to quit smoking, quit drinking, get off addictive drugs; all those bad habits, and it is also used to shed unwanted weight. If that is your goal, be aware that these tough problems do not go away in one cycle. Those ingrained habits that you are deeply married to will need multiple cycles and most likely follow through in the mundane world, such as the seeking of professional help. If you are not seriously ready to give up a habit, spell craft will not work. A way to go about such tough work is to start the spell by asking for the desire to quit the bad habit. By the end of the waning moon, as the moon heads toward darkness again, you are in a position to cleanse again and start a new cycle of energy work using the ever-changing energy of the moon.

By following the steps above with each phase of the moon you can make changes in your life. Just remember that it is a twenty-eight-day cycle so it will not just instantly happen.

The Full Lunar Spell

A full lunar spell should take twenty-eight days. Start on the waxing moon for increasing something or the waning moon for something that you wish to rid from your life. After that you should take time each week to work with the moon in whatever phase it is in to turn the spell into what you want. The full moon usually sees the ultimate affect. If you started with the waxing moon, then by the full moon you should see the increase in your life. On the other hand, if you started on the waning moon, then by the full moon you will see that whatever you are giving up beginning to decrease. This is when the deception of the full moon can be most dangerous because it will be very tempting to stop at that point. Don't! Finish the entire spell until you have reached the same point at which you started.

Exercise
Empowering Yourself Spell

If time and money and love are lacking in your life, here's a full lunar spell that focuses on empowering yourself to draw those things to you. First you cleanse yourself of whatever is blocking the pathway to you. Then, because the path is clear, you are consciously attracting what you need to make those things, love or money, more available to you. This spell takes a full month and, therefore, will not be complete until the moon goes through its entire cycle.

You will need: only yourself.

Start the spell on the waning moon, a night or two after the full moon. Use that energy to define what is truly lacking in your life. Usually, it is lack of belief in your own power, your own magick. Over the course of the waning moon let that energy take away your lack of belief.

The night of the dark moon let that energy wash over you. Focus its power into cleansing you of not believing in yourself.

As the moon starts to wax, start filling yourself up with believing that you are powerful. Let your belief grow over this phase. Whenever a negative thought enters your head, remember the night of the dark moon and how it cleansed you.

The night of the full moon is when you go out and feel the fullness of your power. It is time to celebrate you. And do not forget to thank the moon for working with you.

Gibbous Moon

This is a little talked about phase of the moon called the gibbous moon, which appears on the night before it goes full and the night after the actual full moon. At both times the moon appears full, but it is not quite full. There is powerful magick in this phase because it is the shapeshifters' moon. It is a great time to do work that can assist you in your empathic abilities, or your abilities to reach into the world around you as someone or something else. The gibbous moon is not the trickster's moon, but it can turn into that if you try to use the magick without understanding what shapeshifting is. Shapeshifting is the ability to adjust your energy pattern to meet the needs of the situation in which you find yourself. You are still you, but other people perceive you as one of their group.

Everyone has walked into a group of people and immediately felt like they do not fit into that group. It is an uncomfortable feeling, and our first response is normally to hide or simply leave. Working with the gibbous moon can expand your ability to feel what you need to be in those situations. Your empathic abilities will grow. It is that empathy that allows you to quickly adjust your energy to match the energy of that group of people. You can shapeshift into what you need to be to fit in. Learn how to use the energy of the gibbous moon so you can blend into any setting.

Moon Void-of-Course

One last note about the moon: the term *void-of-course* trips up a lot of witches because it can be hard to understand. The expression is tied to the astronomical and astrological movement of the moon and our perspective of the moon as it travels in our sky. The moon in its normal monthly cycle moves through the signs of the Zodiac as they appear in our sky. From our perspective it looks like the moon is actually in each of those star clusters. It is not, of course, but it appears to be doing that, and where magick from an Earth perspective is concerned, it is appearances that count. If you are really working the spell, you will use the Zodiacal energy of whatever the sign the moon is in at the particular point you are in the spell to give the spell an added boost. This is where void-of-course enters the picture.

As the moon moves from one sign to the next it will often go through periods, short ones, where it is not in any sign at all, or it can even appear to move retrograde, or backward. During this period, and most almanacs give you the times, do not do any spellwork at all. Wait until the moon is in one of the Zodiac's constellations to continue your spell. The effects of doing spellwork during a void-of-course can be mild or have no affect at all; or they can be devastating. If the moon is going retrograde, you just might get the opposite of what you wanted. That could be a nightmare if you are trying to heal someone. Use the moon's power to work your magick but always pay attention to the moon and what it is telling you. Regard void-of-course times as periods when the moon is taking a break from all the work we ask of Her.

Solar Energy

In many ways the sun is the exact opposite of the moon. The moon is cool, distant, soft, subtle, and ever changing. It has a deception because its light is only reflective and does not show things clearly on the Earth. On the other hand, the sun is a huge atomic reactor, hot, intense, passionate, and constant. Its light is bright, and nothing can hide in that brilliance. It is the life-giver of this place. Its heat and light are the spark that set all of life here into motion. In most Wiccan traditions the sun is cast as the masculine principle, but there are traditions that view it as feminine.

Solar energies are not as subtle as lunar energies. You are using direct life-giving energy and it is easy to get burned. In any solar drawing down, be aware that you cannot hold this type of energy in its pure form. It must be transmuted into some sort of action. Solar energy does not remain in a stable state. It is the force of change and motion. You cannot store it; it must be used immediately. Overall, solar energies are the energies that you use to spark change and motion into your life, either as part of well-planned spellworking, or just as a bit of a charge when you need to start thinking about getting into action yourself. Use it to encourage growth in your life, especially spiritual growth, awareness, and of course, empowerment.

The sun, like the moon, has different aspects that can be used in different ways, but rather than phases, the energy changes with the times of the day. To be perfectly precise the sun is actually changing, not itself, but its perspective to where you are, minute by minute, so you could structure your drawing down at that level of precision. There are traditions that do recognize very precise times of day for prayers, Roman Catholicism and Islam, for example. The Roman Catholic recognizes seven times of day for prayers: Vigils takes place at 2:00 am; Lauds at 4:30 am; Prime at 6:00 am; Terce at 9:00 am; Sext at 12:00 (noon); Vespers at 4:30 pm; and Compline at 6:00 pm. The Islamic world has five prayer times per day: sunrise, noon, mid-afternoon, shortly after sunset, and just before sleep each night. These are approximate times, based on where you are and how the mechanical clock is working with the actual solar clock. I am a bit too lazy for all of those specifics. Most of us simply recognize three times of day for the sun; rising, noon, and setting. You can, of course, implement any other time of the day if you feel the need, but these three times are a good place to start.

Rising Sun

Let us start where our day starts with the rising sun, which can be used for beginnings of all sorts. This is the perfect energy to apply to any project, plan, dream, hope, desire, wish, or just a vague idea that something ought to be done. This is not the energy to use to implement the plan; this is the energy you use to spark it into motion, sort of like a spark plug gets the whole engine going.

Do not look to the rising sun for any sort of clarity. That is for other energies. The rising sun is for the beginning of understanding, sometimes it is for helping you to see that you are having a problem. This is not the clarity of solution, but the first light shining on a problem, or better yet, a potential problem. This is the moment when you understand that you have work to do. You can begin to get an idea about how to address the issues in your life. This is the place to ask for guidance in setting up a strategy.

The moment the sun crests the horizon in the morning, and if you have never seen it, do so, is one of the most powerful moments in the day. It is the moment when all of life begins again to the new day. In actuality most living things begin to respond to the heat before the light is even visible, which can be felt before sunrise. Think about the power of that. A heavenly body so strong that it gets a response before it even enters the room. Take advantage of that power in your life. The easiest way to do so is to witness a sunrise. Get up a good hour before the light is visible and watch the world come to wakefulness and then draw down the energy of the rising sun, beginning your day with the knowledge that all things can be conquered. That is power, and it is the power that you can use to start to take control of your own pathway.

Noon Sun

Only mad dogs and Englishmen go out in the Noon Day Sun, or so the old saying goes. If I had to choose any cosmic force that so completely represented the fullness of power, it would be the sun at noon. For those of us who have spent our lives in the Deep South of the United States, it is the sun that sends us hiding and running for cover. It can give life and it can take it away. Its intensity is a blessing and a curse. If you choose to do a noon solar drawing down, be very careful about getting burned, figuratively and literally and, if hosting a group ritual, be conscious of the skin sensitivities of others. Provide sunscreen and water. Remember, the sun burns indiscriminately. Do not make that part of your ritual.

What do you use the noonday sun's energy for? Consider the sun's two primary purposes, light and heat, and you have your answer. I will start with light. The sun sheds light on the world and it can shed light into your world. It can help you discover things that are hidden or secret. Anything you want exposed can be brought out into the open under the noon sun. If you want a truth spell, here is your answer. It can be used effectively on other people, situations, or on yourself, to find out what your own motivations are, or the dark places inside yourself, where you like to hide, and keep yourself locked up. If the rising sun sheds light on a problem, the noon sun brings clarity to the issue, because nothing can hide under the noon sun.

Now for the heat. Need to add some passion to your life? Use the noonday sun energy. I mean passion generically, not just sexual passion, although that is good, too. It is up to you to decide where the energy goes. Put it into anything in your life that is suffering from lack of attention, and you need to care about in order to complete. This is the passion of motion and activity. If you need a boost to get going, reach for that endless source of energy in the sky and it is yours, and it is free. You can have it in a few minutes. Just remember, do something with it, or it can turn on you and just make you restless, at the very least.

A last word about noon sun energy, there is also a death energy component. There can always be too much of a good thing. Have you ever seen fields after too much sun and not enough clouds? That can happen to you and your psyche as well. The noon sun forces out secrets and brings things into the light. This energy can dry things out. It can burn things up. Be careful when you use it. Especially be careful if any other person is involved. The same goes for the heat. If you need passion and motion, then go for it, but remember just how much energy is available and do not burn yourself up by taking more than you need. A rule of thumb is that if you want to use noon sun energies for passion or clarity, have someone else available to assist you, if possible, until you are sure you can make the judgments yourself.

Setting Sun

Because most of us live apart from the classic agricultural lifestyle, we tend to see far more sunsets than sunrises. I doubt that you or anyone has failed to be impressed with the beauty and majesty of the sun as it sets. It is the time of day to say goodbye, close up shop, go home, and prepare for the coming night. In times past the setting of the sun was the signal to go hide away for the night because the life-giver was gone, and the mysteries of the night were in charge until the sun returned.

In that aspect the energy of the setting sun is one of goodbyes, and often, fear. This is the perfect energy to let go of your fear of your true self, your own power. That fear is common to most people of power. It is also what keeps us, and you, from using the fullness of our power to enrich ourselves and the world around us.

There is a softness to this energy that is not present in the other two. It is the energy to use for anything that is coming to, or has been, completed. The setting sun can be used to set a project on its way with a blessing. This is the perfect energy to use to say farewell. If you have a parting coming up or a major change facing you, like moving homes, then this is the time of the day during which you prepare yourself to make the break. The setting sun's energy will provide emotional and spiritual clarity. Ask the sun to assist in your farewells and it will ease the way.

At some point in your life, either you or someone you care for, will need assistance in the mourning process. Whether the loss is a person, a familiar, a job, a dream, it does not matter, if there is pain in the parting, then this is the celestial energy to draw down to assist in the mourning. Do not misunderstand, the setting sun does not make the pain of parting go away, merely makes it easier to say goodbye and gives you, or whoever you are assisting, a safe place to express your emotions. Use the setting sun's energy to say farewell cleanly and to let go of whatever you have lost so that there are no hidden emotions that can bite you on the butt later. Mourning is part of life, and this is a way to mourn with grace and dignity.

Daily Solar Cycles versus Seasonal Solar Cycles

The sabbats are built around the progression of our planet around the sun, which is what produces the seasons and the Wheel of the Year. The daily solar cycles are built around our planet's spinning on its axis. Both the daily cycles and seasonal cycles rely on the sun's energy. Therefore, solar spells can take on two totally different aspects. For drawing downs, use the daily movements of the sun in our sky. This type of spellwork is excellent for things you need to address on the more superficial aspects of life. However, for deep internal work, you can use the power of the sun on the Wheel to work through each phase of that spell as the Wheel turns from season to season.

Exercise
Cleaning the Closet Spell

You can use the daily cycle of the sun to assist you in self-empowerment. If you are really feeling low and a month-long lunar spell just takes too long, or a year-long seasonal working will not affect changes you need right now, the power of the sun can be used fully in a short twenty-four-hour period.

You will need: only yourself.

We all have closets that periodically need cleaning. Now, imagine your life is a closet. You can use the power of the sun and its cycles to assist you to clean this particular closet. Do each part of the spell at the time of that part of the sun's cycle. Just take a few minutes at that time of day and let that aspect of the sun do its job.

Step One: Get up before dawn and use the rising sun to notice that the closet needs to be cleaned. That growing light is showing you the clutter that has accrued. All that junk that is keeping you from being powerful in your own life.

Step Two: When the noon sun arrives let it light up every corner of the closet. Nothing can hide now. That light shows you what needs to be cleaned out. Then let that heat burn away all the things that do not empower you.

Step Three: Let the setting sun take things away from you, things you no longer need. Use the setting sun to say farewell to that which is no longer needed, and you are tossing away.

Midnight Sun

Before moving beyond the sun, I must mention one last solar aspect that is not mentioned often outside of high ceremonial magick circles. It is one that needs to be mentioned because it can be used in a very different way than the solar aspects mentioned. This is the hidden sun. If the daytime sun represents your outer self—the face you show the world—the midnight sun is your hidden self. The sun not showing itself presents an opportunity to do several things. First, without the glaring light of the day, you can show your other faces to the world. These faces often get hidden in what you think you should be, or what you have to pretend to be to please the external situation in which you find yourself. Use the midnight sun to stay true to other parts of yourself as part of maintaining a connection to your internal power.

This is also a great time to set in motion a twenty-four-hour solar spell that will shed light on your inner self. This is especially good if you need to make your external world be more reflective of your internal world. In other words, use this energy to start a solar spell that will assist in integrating your emotions, psyche, and body. Start with the hidden part of you that is journeying on the other side of the world in the darkness, then get up and see the sun rise. Thank the sun for returning and start shedding light on the you that is who you really are.

Stellar Energy

You look up into the night sky and see an endless presentation of stars. Like diamonds scattered across a huge piece of velvet, the stars twinkle and shine and call out to you. You feel compelled to draw their energy down into yourself, but you are perplexed as to what exactly that energy is. Here is something that might help.

When you see a star, what are you looking at? You are looking at the suns of the universe, but this is not the same energy as that of our sun. Why? Stellar light is actually very old light. Technically you are looking at those suns as they were in the past. Therefore, the stars are gateways to the past. Drawing down their energy assists you in travels to different times, especially your own past lives. Use the energy to explore who you have been, so you can better understand who you are. Do not become so enamored with who you were that you stop living in this time.

Stellar energy can give you a whole new perspective on age-lessness, age, and getting old yourself. The energy can be used to ease someone's transition into the Crone or Sage phase of life, because the stars are timeless, and they have seen it all. Their wisdom comes from having seen little planets like ours, and little creatures like us, come and go. The stars are windows into the past and they remind us that the cosmos is eternal.

One cautionary note: we make a lot of jokes about not mistaking a plane or satellite for a star and drawing it down into the backyard, but it can happen. Be careful. Make sure your star is actually a star before drawing down its energy.

Exercise
Who Have I Been?

Past life regression through meditation is discussed more thoroughly in Chapter Nine. There are other ways to explore your past selves. Use tarot cards or cast a spell.

You will need: only yourself.

Choose whichever method with which you feel comfortable. Incorporate the power of the stars by beginning the process with a stellar drawing down. Ask this cosmic energy to guide you through your own past selves.

When you are finished, thank the power of the stars for lighting your way through your past selves. Thank those past selves, too. They took time from the life they were living to come and chat with you.

Planetary Energy

The universe is full of planets. Potentially you could draw down planetary energy from anywhere, but it is so much easier to use the energy of the planets in our own little solar system. If nothing else, there is a bit of history and tradition surrounding these, and some sense of what each one can be used for. They are an ever-present influence in our own part of the universe. If you are familiar with astrology, then you already understand how the planets have a daily effect on each of us and even perhaps how you can use their energy as part of a drawing down.

It is difficult to discuss planetary energy in a general sense since each planet is distinct. It is always advisable to zero in on the specific planet, or combination of planets whose influence you would like to have as a constant in your life. Remember these are constant energies. Once you get their attention, it takes a while to make it go away. Best done by drawing down only one at a time; or if you really need to, a carefully thought-out combination.

Planetary energies work extremely well for self-empowerment. To use them effectively you need to do the research about which planets have the aspects you want to develop inside yourself. If you are struggling with feeling unattractive, Venus is the planet to call into action. However, it is not self-empowering to ask Venus to make you more attractive. It is much more empowering to request that you see yourself as attractive and to believe that you are attractive. Instead of changing something external to you or how the world sees you, you are changing how you see yourself. Venus will assist with that goal.

If you are struggling at your job to be taken seriously. This is a good time to combine two planetary energies. Call on Jupiter to assist you in believing you have value at your workplace. Then ask Mercury to make your communication skills more diplomatic so others are willing to listen to you. If you want an extra boost, you can ask Saturn to give you the discipline you need to bide your time and unveil your value at the job when you are in the height of your power. Again, self-empowerment is not about changing others. It is all about changing how you view yourself.

Planetary Energies

The following is a list of each planet and a few of the energies with which it is most often associated:

Mercury: communication, speed, sexual ambiguity, sometimes medicine, learning, scholastic endeavors (but not long-term retention), messages, business, thievery

Venus: love (of all types), beauty, relationships, social settings, hosting, emotional communication

Mars: sexual passion, aggression, war, victory, dancing, daring, courage, warrior, combat

Jupiter: joy, jollity, money, success, wisdom, thunder, dignity, judicial proceedings, justice, leadership

Saturn: teaching (especially spiritual), death and rebirth, time (and all time-based magicks), history, religious quests, discipline, and history

Uranus: electricity, unpredictability, revolution, changes, freedom, originality

Neptune: mysticism, addictions, imprisonment, deception, visions, illusions, idealism

Pluto: wealth, transformation, power, control

Retrograde Periods

Keep in mind that planets all need a break from our requested work every now and then. Those breaks take the form of that planet going retrograde, similar to the moon. As noted earlier, retrograde means that, from our perspective, the planet appears to be moving backward. Each planet has its own retrograde cycle. The big outer planets go retrograde for long periods of time, while the inner planets have much shorter retrograde periods.

Retrogrades are often regarded as negative times, because people do not want to readjust to the planet's effects. However, I take retrograde periods to review, reassess, rework, and realign with whichever set of energies that particular planet rules. Retrograde is a great time for reflection, not action. When Venus is retrograde, it is not the time to get a facelift. It is the time to do a whole lot of thinking about that facelift. You can also use the energy of retrogrades to improve your next actions, so that you are completely ready to go forward when the planet goes forward.

Comet Energy

They come from far away, hang in our reality for a while, then travel on to someplace else. Comets are the travelers of the cosmos, and their energy can be used to invoke change in your life. This type of change usually involves travel, either yourself or someone else who is traveling through your life. That someone can have a profound effect on you, even if you do not catch their name.

Use cometary energy if you are looking to change directions, travel to new places, move in new directions. Be aware, however, the changes that comets bring are complete and permanent. If you have any death energy already in you, that could lead you your own demise. Cometary drawing downs can attach to that and have a devastating effect. Be prepared, clear, and ready for changes before you draw down this energy. If you just randomly draw down cometary energy, you are inviting change into life without direction. The energy will go to the area of least resistance and force change in that area, whether that area needs change or not. Before drawing down comet energy, be very clear on your intent and focused on which area of your life you wish to change. And, as a precaution, be aware of any weaknesses in your life because changes will occur in those places first.

Meteor Energy

Hurtling across the night sky, burning brightly, then gone, is a shooting star or meteor. If you have ever made a wish on a falling star, then you have drawn down meteor energy. Brief and intense, this energy is best used for short-term changes of focus, lighting up a new pathway of interest, or just applying a little celebratory energy to your life. Like the meteor itself, this energy burns brightly and then is quickly gone. Do not depend on it for permanent changes.

A whole shower can be used in the same way, just with a very intensified quality. If you decide to draw down energy from a meteor shower, do not go in with a shopping list of changes you want to affect. Better to take all of your immediate wants and encapsulate them with a one- or two-word focus, then apply the energy for an overall effect.

Move fast, take advantage of the energy burst while it is still there. Like the meteor, it will soon be gone.

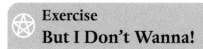

Exercise
But I Don't Wanna!

There is a trip coming up in your life. You really do not want to take this trip. A meteor drawing down is perfect to make a quick change in those travel plans.

You will need: only yourself.

Draw down the energy and ask that the trip be canceled. Be precise on ways to get it canceled. You do not want to cause harm to anyone, or to yourself. Catching a cold might keep you from having to make the trip, but do you really want to sneeze for a week? You no longer want to date that person. Refocus their attention using meteor energy. A big family dinner is planned at your house on a really bad day. A meteor drawing down can cause just enough of an upset in someone's schedule that the date of the dinner has to be changed.

Earth Energy

Earth energy is the one energy that we all forget about. We are so used to taking the Earth's energy for granted that we often fail to use that energy in a focused and intentional way. The Earth's energy is available to us to be used as part of a drawing down. Where the Earth is concerned, however, it is more appropriately a drawing up. Unless you are using that energy to ground yourself, which is when you send your energy into the Earth to allow the Earth to stabilize you.

We are part of this place, the Earth, and its energy courses all around us and through us. Many things in our world are aimed at separating us from this very basic energy, but the more you separate, the more unhappy you will become. That unhappiness can take many forms: disease, money problems, lack of satisfactory relationships, and all because you have disengaged your soul from the most basic energy of all, the Earth. Plants and animals live each moment to its fullest because they do not have all that interference between them and the energy of the Earth all around them.

Empower yourself by drawing the energy of the Earth into yourself. Call upon the power of the Earth when you just need to fill yourself with the power of the natural world. Another way to use the earth energy is when something needs to grow in your life. If you need money, ask the Earth to share its amazing gift of nurturing. The same is true for love. However, the best type of growth you can ask for the Earth's assistance with is growth within you.

———————

All of the types of drawing downs listed above began with the drawing down of the full Moon. That particular esbat is the most basic of a witch's handbook. Most beginning witchlings start with that one. It is certainly the one that has gotten a lot of press. However, all those other energies are part of the cosmos. A discerning witch can be working on a Wheel of the Year spell and also add any of these energies if the need arises.

Chapter Three
TOOLS AND ELEMENTS

Witches often use a long list of tools in their magick and rites. At this stage of your evolution as a witch or Wiccan you do not need a detailed list or description of all those tools. After you have gathered and worked with some of those tools, the next step is claiming your personal power through the way each tool resonates with you. Increasing your resonance with each tool empowers you and your magick. And always remember that the most important tool, of course, is yourself.

Each of the quarter tools has an element attached to it and I find it hard to discuss one without the other. Those elements are a reflection of the natural world around us. Reality is created when the elements come together. Take the time to look at how the elements work in the environment. Put down the magick book for a few minutes and think about the natural world. The magickal elements work in the same way that the natural elements do. Air blows around and creates wind, or it sits stagnant and becomes uncomfortable. Fire is the warming heat of the hearth, or a raging inferno that cleanses everything in its way. Water can be anything from a lovely babbling brook to a tsunami that washes away a lot of debris. Earth is the solid ground beneath your feet, or it is an earthquake that shakes up solid reality. That knowledge empowers any working you do with the elements from a magickal perspective, and your magickal tools help make that happen.

The Basics

Different Wiccan traditions associate tools with the elements in different ways. The one that is most often seen with variations are the wand and the athame, both of which can be associated with air or fire. Therefore, in ritual circumstances, these tools may be in different quarters. While the elements are specific to the quadrant that they call home, the truth is each tool can be used in any quadrant and should be used as appropriate for the magickal working that you are doing. In the end, it is up to the witch to decide elemental associations and where to place their tools. Always follow your instincts and what works best for you. Here is how I do it.

Wand and Air

The East is the home of air. Air is an essential component of our natural world. The movement of air through our atmosphere is what begins all weather patterns, for good or for ill. Wind is air in motion. Air also carries sound, which is why space is soundless. There is no air in space. Lest we forget, air is also required for most life on this planet. We humans require air to breathe.

Every time you have been stressed and someone told you, or you told yourself, to just breathe, you were using the element of air. Calming yourself is a way of taking control of your power. You can do this even more effectively by consciously using air to empower yourself in all situations. Before you react, use air to cleanse yourself of any negative emotions. Once you are cleansed, you can act rather than react. That is expressing your will into a situation.

I use the wand in the east. It is a tool that points my way into a new adventure. However, if using the athame in the east and the wand in the south suits you more comfortably, then by all means, do so. Use your wand to pull the power of air into you. You can do this during a formal ritual. You can also do it if you just need that power in a moment. Grab your wand and use it to direct your will into the air so it can move to whatever goal you wish. Like the wind blowing across the earth, your will can become a force of nature that starts the creation of your desired reality.

Athame and Fire

The south is the home of fire. Fire is another essential component of our natural world. Fire is a catalyst that creates things by burning off impurities or melding other substances together to create something new. Fire gives us heat and light.

You use the power of fire every time you crank your vehicle. The spark plug sets the engine in motion. You can use the power of fire to empower yourself in just the same way. If you are having trouble getting started on something in your life, call on the fire within you to spark the engine of your life into motion. Then move, get into action. Let fire ignite your desire to create the reality you desire.

I use the athame in the south. This is the tool that cuts through obstacles. However, if using the wand in the south suits you more comfortably, then by all means, do so. Use your athame to slice through your own hesitations about taking action. You can create any reality you desire once you have sparked yourself into action.

Chalice and Water

The west is the home of water, another component of our natural world. Water is the most mysterious of the elements because it has so many secrets. It is water that makes life possible here. All living things on this planet, from the smallest microbe to the penultimate, humans, require water to live. Aside from that mystery, water is unique in something else. It is the only substance that we know of that naturally goes through all three states of matter: gas, liquid, and solid.

One of the areas of our lives that we keep the most secret is our emotions. Sometimes we even hide feelings from ourselves. You can empower yourself greatly by using water to wash away barriers you have created to hide from your own emotions. Whether you take a shower or a hot bath, or just go out and let rain cleanse you, use the power of water to set your emotions free. Once you have embraced even the darkest of emotions, you are free to let those emotions go. That letting go will free up space inside you for new, and hopefully, positive emotions.

The chalice holds things, even secrets. Fill your chalice with water. Add salt if you wish. Some witches add salt so they have a water/earth combination to bless the circle when they cast it. My preference is to keep each element pure to itself. As always, follow your intuition and what works best for you. Look deep into that chalice. Seek out your own secrets, the ones that are creating blocks inside you. Those blocks, secrets, are keeping you from reaching the depth of your own power. Once you have seen the secrets and when you are ready to admit them to yourself, toss the water to the ground. Rinse the chalice and add fresh water. Use that to create a reality where you keep no secrets from yourself. The truth you tell yourself is a life giving and empowering force.

Pentacle and Earth

The north is the home of earth. It is earth upon which we stand so it is an essential component of our natural world. Soil, rocks, trees, plants, all the elements of the solid world are where reality starts and ends.

Ask anyone who gardens, and they will tell you that there is great comfort in just touching dirt. The earth is a tremendous source of stability. Any time you are feeling unsettled or unsure, just grab a handful of dirt. Hold it, clutch it, smell it. You can feel life in it, but yet it is stable. Feel the ground beneath your feet. Let the roots of who you are extend into the earth. Then let all that lack of surety flow into the earth through those roots. Let the earth stabilize you so you can create a reality that is filled with your essence.

I use the pentacle as the tool of the north. Often that pentacle is engraved on a platter of some sort. In ritual, I might serve food off that platter to nourish our bodies—another symbol of earth. The pentacle is also a shield that has the ability to protect you from the blows of life. Sometimes we feel unstable because life has just smacked us around. Hold up your pentacle; let the power of the earth take the blows for a bit. You will feel safe and strong behind that shield. When your body has regained its strength, the strength of the earth, your reality will be more stable.

 Exercise
Mapping Out a New Plan

It is time to plan something out; a quest for a new job, a summer vacation, a magickal working, whatever. You want to make sure you get started with a good map of the journey.

You will need: a pencil or pen, a piece of paper, your tools for each element; be sure you have some water or whatever you prefer in your chalice.

This exercise is aimed at creating that map. You can do this in one sitting, or you can do it over a period of days. The first step is to cast a circle.

Next, put your paper and writing implement in front of you. Take your wand and turn to the east. Call on air to point you in the right direction. Mark an X on the paper to indicate this is where you are, your starting point. Mark another X somewhere on the other end of the paper to indicate your goal. You can even write that goal down, in a few words, next to the X. Lay your wand on the paper. Let its power of direction fill you and the paper. Start drawing lines from you to your goal. Don't worry if it isn't a straight line, or if there are lines that go nowhere. Just draw until you have a line from your starting point to your goal. Put your wand to the east of the paper.

Take your athame and turn to the south. Call on fire to point out any obstacles you will meet as you move toward your goal. Mark each place with an X. When you have accounted for each possible obstacle, take your athame and stab those Xs so you are enforcing your will over any obstacle.

Take your chalice and turn to the west. Call on water to fill you with faith in yourself and your journey. Take a sip and then set the chalice on the emerging map. Look at those obstacles again and for each one, take a sip and renew your faith in your ability to get past that bump in the road.

Take your pentacle and turn to the north. Call on earth to see your goal attained. Put the pentacle on the map. Place it so that the top point sits directly on the X that marked the end of the journey. Touch the pentacle and see that you have attained your goal.

When your map is complete, open your circle. Place the map in a safe space, preferably on your altar. Once you have reached your goal, you can dispose of the map however you wish.

Cauldron and the Center

Once you have all the elements put together inside you, it is time to take your power at the center. The center is the place where all the elements combine to create reality. It is where we place the cauldron. Into the cauldron flows all potential and out of it flows what has been created from that potential.

You in the fullness of your power are the cauldron at the center. The air you breathe; the fire that is your passion; the water is your emotions, blood, and tears; the earth is your body. Together they combine to create you. Feel all those elements inside you. Stir them all up together in yourself. Use your imagination to pour that reality out into the world. It is the reality you have created by using the power of the elements to empower yourself.

The cauldron we use at the center is the classic witch's cauldron, although in myth it has a reputation that is far from the truth. The cauldron represents all that is reality and has the power to create reality. You, as the cauldron, are the creator of your own reality.

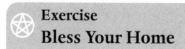

Exercise
Bless Your Home

Your home is an extension of you. Whether you have a house, an apartment, or a single room, that is your home. You can turn it into a permanent standing sacred space by using the elements to bless it. Your power will infuse your space if you draw on your internal connection to the elements.

You will need: each of your tools, including your cauldron.

Start by casting a circle.

Next, face east. Rather than use incense to pull air into the East, use your own breath. Blow your essence of the mind and imagination into that area.

Face south; there is no need to light a candle now. Ignite the flame of your own courage inside yourself and let that fire fill this area of your home.

Face west; water is a major component of your body. That is all you need to let the power bless this area of your home.

Face north; your body and its strength are the earth you use in this area. Infuse this area with your own strength. Stamp your foot and see the shock waves fill the area.

Return to the center. Let all that is your connection flow in all directions of your home. Your power has now consecrated your space. You can open your circle.

Exercise
Connecting to a Storm

Storms are made up of air, water, and fire. So, they are an excellent way to connect several elements together. You can link those three elements back to the earth through yourself, effectively becoming the center that will connect the elements. Storms tend to clear the atmosphere, so they are good sources for revitalizing or refreshing yourself or anything around you. When you are feeling stormy, you can use the elements from inside you to clear your own turbulence. I do recommend that you do this one outdoors if at all possible. You may well call up a storm in the world around you.

You will need: each of your quarter tools, be sure there is something drinkable in your chalice.

Cast a circle. Let the storm build inside you by pulling the elements of air, water, and fire together. Hold your wand and take deep breaths. Hold your athame and draw lightning strikes through the air. Drink deeply from your chalice letting your body fill with water.

When you are peaking in your internal storm, let it break out of you. Breathe hard and stir the air with your wand. See lightening draw to that athame. If possible, splash some of the water in your chalice to the ground. Your own body as the earth will shake, rattle, and roll for a bit. However, when the clouds inside you break and the storm is over, you will be refreshed and revitalized. Open your circle.

Using the Elementals

Typically, when witches learn the laundry list of correspondences for the four quarters, we learn the elemental being associated with the direction: sylphs in the east, salamanders in the south, undines in the west, and gnomes in the north. As our connections to each element grows and we become more proficient in building magickal circles, many witches tend to stop making the long calls that include all the many associations. Often some of what goes by the wayside is the elemental beings that exist and rule each element. Those entities should remain in your repertoire no matter how proficient you get, because they can be extremely useful working partners. Here are some of the ways you can work with the elementals:

Sylphs
If you need to know something of an intellectual nature, ask sylphs to go through air and gather the data you require. I do not recommend that you use sylphs to cheat on an exam or your taxes. Their perspective is different from ours and you might get accurate information, but precision is lacking.

Salamanders
If you are angry with someone but cannot bring yourself to enter into a confrontational situation, call for some salamanders to help you get past the anger and find your own courage. Sylphs can assist here, too, but they can make you more diplomatic in your approach and find the right words. Salamanders, because they are fire elementals, are less likely to try to be friendly. They will express your thoughts more directly without concern for what the response will be.

Undines
As you probe deep inside yourself to uncover your own secrets, call on undines to dive with you. They are not afraid of the depths,

and they know the mysteries of the water. They can show where to swim inside yourself.

Gnomes

Having issues connecting to your own body? Gnomes are strong creatures who understand all the interactions of the material world. Call on their assistance in defining what you need to do to properly align your material essence so your body can correct itself.

Elemental Messages

Using elementals to send messages requires some concentration on your part. Focus on which elemental or elementals will work the best to send the message. If you are sending a message to another person, it works extremely well to send the elemental of their sun sign. Need to let an Aries, Leo, or Sagittarius know something? Send salamanders. If you do not have that information, default to sylphs because of their connection to air and the East.

Whether casting a circle or sending a message, working with the elementals is also working with the elements of our natural world. What you are doing in essence is empowering yourself by strengthening your connection to those elements. The stronger those connections are, the more you can affect the reality around you. Make sure the connection stays friendly by always saying thank you to any elemental with which you have worked. They, like us, enjoy knowing their efforts were appreciated.

Exercise
Wish You Hadn't Said That

Someone who is threatened by you and your power has started spreading rumors about you. Facing them down directly will cause problems in your social network. Now is the time to send an elemental to convey a message. You can send sylphs just to convey a message, or you can send a salamander to let them know that the witch is angry. They will not realize the message came from you. They will just know that they should stop talking about you.

You will need: whatever tool and element is required for that particular elemental; for this one your athame, a fire source—candle or brazier.

Choose which elemental and the appropriate tool for that elemental. I'm going with salamanders, so I would use an athame.

You can cast a formal circle or just focus on the quarter to which that elemental is attached, in this exercise, fire.

Light a candle or a fire in your brazier. Focus on the flames and visualize the salamanders inside the flame.

Call out to the salamanders and get their attention. Ask them to do you a favor. You will know they are willing when they look back at you in a friendly way. Sometimes they even nod a little.

Tell them what has happened and who did it. Send a clear mental image of that person to them with the name.

Ask them to let that person know you are angry and that the talking about you should stop.

Thank the salamanders and send them on their way.

Put out whatever fire you used and if you cast a circle, open it.

Using Tools Outside the Circle

The working tools of each element exist in this reality, but they also have an astral existence. How deep your connection is to each element, and thus to each tool can be gauged by how quickly you can call up the tool in the astral if you have need of that tool. If you find yourself needing the protection of your pentacle in a social or professional situation, then call on it. The stronger your connection to the pentacle, the north, and the earth, the more powerfully you will feel its presence. The same is true of all the tools. They are the conscious and subconscious symbols of the elements. You have invested each with your power. Make that power count on all planes of reality. Once you have done that you have access to the tools and what they represent across the realities as well.

What happens when someone else touches or handles your tools? If you have given them permission, then it is perfectly okay. The issue really surfaces when someone just randomly starts playing with, touching, or handling your tools. Many witches, mostly young ones, have a fear that when that happens then the tool will lose some of its magick. Maybe, but what is more likely to happen is that the power in the tool will harm that careless and disrespectful person. Remember tools have their own power and they will fight to defend themselves and their witch.

The tools of a witch are symbols that represent cosmic truths. Each one has its own power, its own identity. However, each one also should bring up much deeper cosmic truths from your subconscious when you see it. As you empower yourself by connecting more deeply to each element, your understanding of the mysteries of that element will grow and reach deeper levels. Every time you see one of your tools, or any sacred tool, your subconscious will begin to reach for a deeper connection to those mysteries. Eventually, those mysteries will not be just in your subconscious, but part of your conscious awareness. You just have to listen, and you will begin to hear the whispers of the tools and what they really represent.

Chapter Four
SACRED SPACE

Creating sacred space as you cast your circle is something you probably have been doing since you picked up your first wand. It is one of the very first things witches learn as they begin their work in Wicca. All religious forms create a sacred space in some way. Wiccans do it by casting a circle. The circle is the basic tool of magick, and it is always around you. It is an expression of your personal power. The circle represents a model of the cosmos and remember this magickal circle is a sphere, not just a flat circle.

There are a variety of types of magick circles, but they all contain similar qualities. They all create a sacred space. Cleansing the old energy normally comes first. Then the space is secured by establishing a boundary. In Wicca we do this by calling the four quarters. Druidic circles call three Watchtowers rather than four. Christian churches usually have someone come in the day before the service and physically clean the church. The sacred space was sanctified at the time of the church's consecration, but it is reinforced at every service with opening prayers and hymns. The style used is ultimately up to the witch who is doing the casting. It must answer your needs and those with whom you are working. An example of how this can work is if you are doing a healing circle.

The person who has asked for healing is not following the Wiccan religion but is actually a Christian. You can cast a Wiccan circle, but at each quarter call to the appropriate Archangel for that quarter. Those names will most likely be familiar to the Christian. Hearing the names, maybe feeling the energy of the archangels, can add a level of comfort for this person. Being more comfortable quite possibly will make them more receptive to the healing spell.

You probably already know how to cast a Wiccan circle, and you can use your own tradition's methods in your quest to strengthen your inner power. In this chapter I am going to review the very basic steps in creating a basic Wiccan sacred space but one that is empowered by you and is not just words on a page.

Cleansing

As in most Wiccan traditions you must first cleanse the space to be used for building your circle. Any time you are in a new space that has never been used or if you are building a circle in a room or outdoor area used for other purposes, cleanse it first so that any power and energy that come into it are from you and your circle alone. You can use a broom to sweep it clean. You can ring bells all around to drive out negative energies.

Cleansing is not always necessary if you have a permanent, standing circle, inside or out. However, if there were any negative energies introduced to the circle, cleanse it as well. Use your intuition about whether it is necessary or not. If you have any doubt in your mind about whether it should be cleansed, then cleanse the space, better safe than sorry.

You should also take a few minutes to cleanse yourself. We all carry negative emotions or thoughts, so take a minute before you start the work to get rid of those negatives. The negatives just block your power because they lead to self-doubt. Sit quietly and do some deep breathing to rid yourself of anything other than the work about to be done. You can use smoke from incense to cleanse. The best two cleansing scents are sage and sandalwood, but if you have a special affinity for a particular scent, use that. You can also sprinkle some water on yourself, or just take a purifying bath or shower ahead of time. The goal is to enter any working feeling your most powerful, full of belief in yourself and your magickal abilities.

Calling the Quarters

After you cleanse yourself and your space, you are ready to cast the circle. Again, you most likely already know how to go to east, south, west, and north and call those pillars, the four quarters, into your reality. You know long lists of correspondences that will assist you in doing those calls. You most likely have become accustomed to thinking of those quarters as something external to yourself. However, you stand at the center of that sacred space. Those four directions and all their correspondences are far stronger if they start from inside you. Your sacred space is you and the projection of your will, your power.

What follows is a very simple list of correspondences for the four directions, the quarters. None of them will be a surprise for you. However, as you review them, think of them as coming from inside you as opposed to external to you. Change the way you visualize the elements.

East: The Element of Air

Where the magick starts for your dreams and goals.

Keywords	The mind, beginnings, imagination, intellect, music, play, whimsy, birth
Circle location	The eastern gate, where souls who are ready to re-enter this living realm of reality come into life
Time of Day	Sunrise
Time of Year	Spring
Colors	Yellow, rose, and light blue
Animals	Eagle, dove, and most birds
Archangel	Raphael
Elemental	Sylphs
Gender	Masculine
Astrological Sign	Gemini, Libra, Aquarius
Sabbats	Ostara and Beltaine occur on the southeast spoke of the Wheel
Tools	Wand, staff, censor, incense. There are some traditions where some of the tools of the East and the South are reversed

South: The Element of Fire

Where the magick is focused by your will.

Keywords	The will, sexual power, courage, desire, lust, strength, the prime of life
Location	The southern gate, where life at its fullest and souls are reaching for totality of experience
Time of Day	Midday or noon
Time of Year	Summer
Colors	Red, orange, yellow
Animals	Lion, dragon, wolf
Archangel	Michael
Elemental	Salamanders
Gender	Masculine
Astrological Sign	Aries, Leo, Sagittarius
Sabbats	Litha and Lughnasa occur on the Southwest spoke of the Wheel
Tools	Athame, sword, fire pit, brazier. There are some traditions where some of the tools of the East and the South are reversed

West: The Element of Water

Where the magick uses your faith and belief to become open.

Keywords	The heart, endings, emotion, belief, faith, heart, leave taking
Location	The western gate is the gate through which the newly departed leave this realm and enter the afterlife
Time of Day	Sunset
Time of Year	Autumn
Colors	Blues, purples, black
Animals	All fishes, porpoises, whales, leviathan
Archangel	Gabriel
Elemental	Undines
Gender	Feminine
Astrological Sign	Cancer, Scorpio, Pisces
Sabbats	Mabon and Samhain occur at the northwest spoke of the Wheel
Tools	Chalice and water; sometimes may include sea salt

North: The Element of Earth

Where the magick becomes reality.

Keywords	The body, stability, strength, becoming part of reality, wealth, the dead
Location	The northern gate, which is approximated to be the home of the Dead because it is here that they prepare for their reentry to the next life
Time of Day	Midnight
Time of Year	Winter
Colors	Brown, green, black
Animals	Bear, bull, sow, behemoth, basilisk
Archangel	Uriel
Elemental	Gnomes
Gender	Feminine
Astrological Sign	Taurus, Virgo, Capricorn
Sabbats	Yule and Imbolc occur at the northeast spoke of the Wheel
Tools	Pentacle, salt, or earth in a container

Exercise
Reaching for the Elements Inside You

Here is an exercise that you can do to start reaching for the power of the quarters inside you. I start in the East because of my early ceremonial training. This is not a requirement at all. Many Wiccans start creating sacred space in the North. Start where you feel you should. Whatever works best for you is the way to go. It is about empowering yourself after all.

You will need: Iincense, a scent that you love. A candle, the color should represent you. A color of your astrological sign works very well. A glass of water, or wine if you prefer. A dish with a little salt in it.

Face the East, the place of air, and take a deep breath. Light the incense. Feel the air flow through your body. Now blow out that air. Blow it out with all the force you can and from deep inside you. See the Eastern Gate open with the power of your will.

Face the South, the place of fire. This one is a bit harder because you definitely do not want to set yourself on fire. Light the candle. Find what you are passionate about. Let that passion be the flame that grows inside you, fills you. When you are ready, imagine your passion, your fire lighting up the Southern Gate.

Face the West, the place of water. Take a sip of the water. Feel your own liquid components flowing through your body, blood of course, but water, too. Let the tide of your own body wash through you and then out of you. Let that tide fill and open the Western Gate.

Face the North, the place of earth. Put a pinch of the salt on your tongue and let it dissolve into your mouth. Feel every part of your body. Let your body connect to the earth beneath your feet. Imagine your body has roots and send those roots to the North and open the Northern Gate.

Complete your circle by facing the East again. Connect with all four quarters and fill your sacred space with your power.

Your sacred space is now yours, not created by external forces. It has been created by your connection to those forces. Stand in the space for as long as you wish and just feel your connections to the elements. When you are ready, ground yourself and the open your circle.

The Circle Center

Creating your sacred space from inside yourself puts your will at the center of the circle and the work. The center of the circle is where all the elements come together. You, as the center, are now the nexus point of the elements. They come together inside you and from you they extend to the entire circle.

Here are a few correspondences for the center itself:

Center: The Home of Spirit

Where you stand as the power of the sacred space.

Keywords	The gestalt, balance, completion, all things crystalized
Location	The center of the circle, however some traditions place it in the north
Time of Day	All hours of the day
Time of Year	The whole year
Colors	Any color that is appropriate to the work at hand
Animals	Any animal if one is needed
Archangel	None
Elemental	None
Gender	Masculine and feminine
Astrological Sign	All twelve
Sabbats	The entire Wheel of the Year
Tools	Cauldron

Opening the Circle

Do not forget that when your working is done you must open the circle. You are used to the practice of thanking each quarter and releasing it to the cosmos. When opening these types of circles, do the same. The difference when you are incorporating the energies inside yourself is that you will keep the piece of the power of each quarter that is part of you. This makes you more balanced and more powerful.

Connecting the energy of each quarter to that aspect of yourself makes you the center of the power. You have effectively become a gestalt of the quarters. The center of a sacred space is the same thing. Once you have opened your circle, the space you created is no longer filled with your power. You, however, are still filled with that energy. The goal is to maintain a balance of the quarters inside you. Do not ground that power out of yourself, but you may need to work on a balancing of the energy. If you are feeling a bit too garrulous or talking too much, eat something. If you want to go out and start a fight, drink a glass of water, juice, or wine. Crying too much? Watch a talkative stand-up comic and laugh. Having trouble just getting up and moving? Light a candle and focus on the flame. Earth balances air; water balances fire; air balances water; fire balances earth. You are using the elements/quarters inside yourself to achieve balance. A balanced witch is a much more powerful witch.

Chapter Five
EMPOWERMENT: SPELLCASTING

Your tools are ready. You can cast a circle. You celebrate the sabbats and esbats. What else do witches do? Cast spells, of course. It is that ability for which witches are most well-known and feared. It is also what draws so many to the path of the witch. It is, however, not as simple, or as easy as it is portrayed. Many people who make fun of witches spend a lot of energy trying to undermine the witch's confidence. One of the biggest ways is when outsiders say that witches are not real. I often wonder why people put so much energy into trying to deny the power of witchcraft. What are they so afraid of? That fear has long made us a target. One of the first spells you do should be to cast a protection spell against that fear and, honestly, the very best protection is simply believing in your own power. Empower and protect yourself against negativity with the confidence of knowing who you are and what you can do.

Energy Flow

What is a spell? A spell occurs when you focus energy to achieve a desired outcome; when you use energy to cause the flow of energy around to bend to your will to create a specific reality of your choice. This is a definition from the Disney movie *Halloweentown* (1998) that sums it up, "Magick is simple. Decide what you want and then let yourself have it."[4] They got it right, almost. Paraphrasing Aleister Crowley, money is only a problem when you start to count it. The key is energy flow and bending that energy to shape reality into what you want the reality to be. Once you count the money, you have stopped the energy flow.

The most effective energy manipulation is when you use your own energy to change yourself. In fact, *the most important spell you will ever cast is the spell that shapes you.* I was taught this long ago, and it is still my guiding principle whenever I plan a spell. How will this spell affect me? The empowerment of the self is an ongoing and continuous lifelong spell and can happen either in a negative or a positive way. Witches believe that we have the ability to create reality as we want it to be and that begins with making yourself what you want to be. Shape reality if you can, but that often comes into conflict with the free will of others, so changing only yourself is usually the most positive way to go. All spells you cast will come back to you threefold, so cast positive spells and you will grow and improve as you work.

Spell Construction: A Review

Ideally all spells start with divination. Many witches will not do any spell without doing some divination to determine whether they should be doing that spell. It is not a bad idea, if for no other reason than to see if it is a true will spell for which you are about to take responsibility. Remember you are responsible for all of your actions. If you cast a spell that hurts you or someone else, then you have no one to blame but yourself. A little divination ahead

---

4 *Halloweentown*, directed by Duwayne Dunham (1998; Disney Channel original movie) 84.

of time will not hurt. There are a multitude of types of divination from tarot to scrying. Use whatever method works best for you.

Once you have decided on your spellworking, you must gather all the appropriate materials. In terms of finding supplies, it is always best to see what turns up or is gifted to you rather than going out and searching for what you have decided is the right thing. Our true will usually know what we need and does not much care what we want.

When gathering those supplies use as many correspondences as possible. The more connections you make, the stronger the spell. Basically, you are stacking the deck of the energy in your favor. Some of the things you will look at are:

Candles: appropriate color and size,
Oils & incense: appropriate scents,
Herbs & natural materials: appropriate to the work and usage,
Cloth (100% natural): type, size, and color for poppets and bags,
String (100% natural): type, length, color.

Correspondences, Correspondences, Correspondences! The more connections you make, the more powerful the spell. Again, you are stacking the deck of the energy in your favor. The correspondences open doorways, externally and internally. They make you more a part of the spell and increase your awareness of what energies you are using to cast the spell. The most important tool you have is yourself. Those correspondences are merging your power with the powers of the cosmos. Empower your magick by letting your subconscious become conscious as you gather the things you need for the spell.

Sometimes you are led to something that appears to be not the right thing. Suppose you are doing a money spell. In most cases, you would reach for anything green to empower the spell but this time your hands, driven by your subconscious, keep grabbing blue. Then go with the blue. In fact, look up the correspondences to blue. Blue is Jupiter's color and odds are that you do not really have a problem with money, but that the energies you need to work with are connected to what Jupiter rules—success and joy. The spell you truly need to cast is to believe that you can achieve and what will follow will be money. Always follow your instinct. It usually knows what it is doing.

Timing

Timing should be thought out very carefully. For growth, use the waxing moon or rising sun. To do a banishing, use the waning moon or setting sun. If a healing spell is required while the moon is waning, then do a banishing of the disease spell. Remember, cast no spells while the moon is void-of-course and never cast a spell of a specific nature to a planetary energy if that planet is in a retrograde period. A spell to increase money flow into your life that is cast while Mercury is retrograde is an open invitation to thieves into your life. Mercury, after all, is the patron deity of thieves.

Sabbats are typically not the appropriate time for individual spells. Sabbats are celebrations for the turning of the Wheel of the Year and the life cycle of the sun. The only exception to that rule is that if you are doing a spell that takes an entire year to do and you have attached that spell to the Wheel of the Year, similar to what I shared in Chapter Two. In fact, I do a Wheel of the Year spell every year and have for I can't remember how long. However, sabbats are celebrations, so do not neglect that aspect of the holy day. The best time to do most spellworking is during an esbat. The esbats are times of work, so you should be casting spells appropriate to that phase of the moon. Just do not forget to thank the moon for the assistance.

Bind and Forget

Once the spell is complete, the final step to all spells, and perhaps the hardest, is to bind the spell and forget it. Binding can be done a variety of ways and most spell books will give you methods. The type of binding usually is a derivative of the type of spell. One way to do this is by reciting, in some form, the Wiccan Rede— *And it harm none, do what you will.* The Rede was first recorded by Doreen Valiente in 1964. You can bind a spell with something like, "By the power of three times three, cause no harm to them or me. As I will it, so mote it be."

And why forget it? As I said, this is often the hardest part of a spell, but it is probably the most important part. We cast a spell for some reason that we believe it is important to focus our will on to get a desired result. In other words, we are married to that situation and give it a lot of power by focusing on it. Once the spell is cast, let it go. Third degree Wiccans and other long-practiced witches do very little spellcasting in a traditional way because they have learned that giving anything that much importance just gives it power. But you have to get to that place first. Cast spells and use them as a catharsis. Once you bind it, let it go and do not think about it anymore. The spell will work itself out and take its own course to completion without any more interference on your part. If you sit around and obsess about it, you will be thwarting the cosmos as it works things out. Bind it and forget it.

There are many differing opinions on how important it is that you believe in the spell. Faith does play a big role, and you should not do any magick if you really do not believe that it will work, but to a certain degree, just going through the motions makes a difference. Always remember the old adage, "Be careful what you ask for, you just might get it." I am never amazed that magick works, but I am often amazed at how it works. The spell will take its own path once you set it free, just be prepared for the results.

Change Yourself, Not Others

Two of the great traps in witchcraft are casting love and money spells. Remember to always aim to change yourself, not someone else. The greatest sin you can commit as a witch is to interfere with someone else's true will. Do not cast spells on someone without their permission. If you have that permission and the spell does not work, assume that their higher self is in charge and deciding what is best for them.

Love spells have an obvious trap when trying to get a specific person to like or love you. You will get that person's attention, and for a while, they will make you the center of their universe, but you will pay a price for interfering with their true will. That price quite often takes the shape of them realizing what has happened and turning on you. They could come to hate you. They could become obsessed with you and start stalking you. At the very least they will eventually stop loving and wanting you, unless you are willing to keep casting the spell all the time, and who wants someone under those conditions.

Empower yourself instead by making yourself more open to love, more willing to believe that you deserve love, and then be able to see the person who loves you because they choose to love you. That is a spell worth casting, and it changes you for the best, and does not interfere with their true will.

As for money spells, well, they can be tough. Typically, it is not money that someone really wants, but an increase in fortune. For a lot of folks, this translates to a desire to set things up so that they do not have to ever work again. That is not magick, it is just plain laziness. How much better is it to appreciate the value of what you do and see the money coming in as a blessing for the skills that you have. Money represents energy flow coming to you. Most often it comes to you because of some special skill or talent you have, or because you have invested your time into something like a job and the money is the payment for that investment. The money shows that what you have done has a value. Money spells work best when you cast them to appreciate yourself what you can do and what you have done and the value of your work.

As you start moving into higher levels of spellcasting, you begin to realize that you are not just projecting your will onto the reality around you. Spellcasting is best done when you start manipulating energy to flow into you and then flow out of you. The energy moves in a circular motion. You pull it into you and freely let it flow out of you. Or the reverse, send the energy out of you and allow it to flow back to you. Ask, believe, receive are the guiding principles of higher-level spellwork. We usually have no trouble asking. Over your years as a witch, you most likely have come to believe that magick works. Receiving is often the hardest part of the spell. Do you truly believe that you deserve that for which you are asking? Do you believe that you deserve to be loved? Do you believe your work deserves to be rewarded? Ask yourself those questions and then put together the right spell to open you up to receiving that for which you have asked. Then believe that you deserve it.

Exercise
Empowering Yourself
Spell Preparation

Regardless of what type of spell you are casting, here is a blueprint for putting together a working so that you are empowering yourself to receive what you need, rather than working on the outside world. Note that you will use a white candle, because you are working on yourself as the center of reality where all colors combine.

You will need: a divination method, a white candle of any size, maybe a piece of paper and a pen or pencil.

Use your choice of divination to define what you need and also what is keeping you from believing you deserve to have whatever you need. It is perfectly okay to create a little cheat sheet of your needs. It can be the focus you use during the divination.

Cast a circle as described in Chapter Four or one in your tradition.

Light the candle and begin a silent meditation. Go deep into yourself. Ask your guides within and without—elements or elementals, deities, or higher self—to show you why you deserve to receive this gift. Witches who are experienced in doing this type of meditation will tell you that the answer may take a bit to come to you, but it will come if you allow yourself to be open to hearing it.

After you have your message, open your circle.

Exercise
Empowering Yourself Spell

With the information that you received during your preparation you can put together the appropriate spell that will open you to receiving this gift. I'll use finding a job as an example.

Let's say you want a new job because you hate the one you have. However, the answer that came to you in meditation told a different story. The truth is that you took the current job only because you did not believe you deserved something better, a job more fitting to your talents. The spell you need to cast is not one for a new job, but rather one that will increase your belief in your talents that transfer easily into the job market.

You will need: staying specific to the spell outlined below—Jupiter correspondences—a blue candle and the appropriate incense; Mercury correspondences—an orange candle and the appropriate incense; Venus correspondences—a green candle and the appropriate incense.

Start by choosing the appropriate energies with which to work. Jupiter should be obvious because he rules success, but he also rules joy. You want to be joyous in your work. Mercury also leaps to mind. That energy can assist you in defining your talents in such a way that they are most appealing in your job search. Finally, add Venus. No energy can assist your more in believing in yourself.

Next check the timing. Always first look to see if any of those planets are in retrograde. Check the phase of the moon, as well. In my example, you are not actually calling on her, but you want to stack the deck in your spell. Since you are defining something within yourself, you want to get as close to the new moon as possible. Planetary days and hours matter, too. Remember, this about empowering yourself and your belief in yourself, so Friday, Venus's day, might be best. The planetary hour could be either Jupiter or Mercury. Since you are shedding light on some hidden part of yourself, also consider the hour of the sun.

Cast your circle.

Call each planetary energy to assist your quest. Call each one separately, lighting the corresponding candle and incense as you make that call. Keep your focus on how the power of that energy can empower you.

Keep your conscious awareness focused on your spell that will make you open to receiving what you need. Let those planetary energies connect with their matching aspect within you.

Bind the spell and forget it. Extinguish each candle as you thank that planetary energy and release it.

Open your circle and get on with your life. Notice the differences in you as you take more pride and joy in your own skills and talents. And watch what doors open for you in the next few weeks.

Blood Magick

One of the most powerful natural materials is blood. There are lots of warnings out there cautioning you against using blood in magick, mainly because it has so often been portrayed as being used in a negative way. And you should be very careful using your blood or anyone else's blood in a spell. Blood binds you to the spell at the cellular level and that is serious. If you use blood to bind you to a spell that you are casting for someone else, then you will be bound to that person. If you are working magick on yourself, your own blood can bind the spell to you more closely, more than the average spell. Sexual fluids, semen, and menstrual blood fall into this category as well, so use these bodily fluids with great care. Binding yourself to a spell at this level has the benefit of making it part of your physical being. The spell will be working and flowing through you at all times—while you're sleeping, at work, feeding the cat—always. Your head may not be thinking of the spell, but your body always is. The spell becomes part of you. If you are doing the spell for someone else, you will be connected to them at the same level. Make sure they know that. I do not recommend blood spells for those who are just beginning their witchy journey. Get some experience at spellcasting in general first.

You do not need a cupful of blood; a drop will do. A small pinprick to your finger will yield all the blood you need. It is that powerful. Just get a small pin. I have a packet of sterile lancets I bought at a pharmacy. They work the best because that is what they are designed to do. Make sure the needle is clean and sterile, so you don't get an infection. The same rule applies if you are using someone else's blood, gather it safely and with consent. If you are doing a spell where you are combining the blood of people, then gather the blood from each person with separate lancets and put a drop of blood in a receptacle of some to combine. As dramatic as it looks in movies and television, slicing and clasping hands is not advisable. It is not necessary to work powerful magick and it certainly isn't safe for the health of the people involved.

When is it appropriate to do a blood spell? Bindings come to mind immediately. You have created an amulet to increase your belief in yourself. You intend to carry the amulet with you. It is a perfect time to add a drop of your blood to the amulet when you empower the amulet during the spell. Two or more people have made the decision that they wish to bind themselves to each other. A blood spell will accomplish that. It is often part of a coven binding. You will also occasionally see it in handfastings. Someone has decided to protect another person, often a child. A blood binding has the ability to increase the internal alarm system in the protector, so they know when the other person is in some sort of jeopardy. No matter what the reason, always deeply consider whether blood should be added to a spell.

Protecting & Cursing

Here is another controversial topic: cursing. Witches have been accused of doing this type of spell since time immemorial and, to a certain degree, rightly so. Yes, we do have that power. We can and do cast curses, because sometimes that is what is needed. This is one area in which preparatory divination plays a critical role. Is the curse necessary? Ask the question and receive the answer. Or, if nothing else, take a minute to review your emotional state. Do not cast curses in the heat of the moment. After you have cooled down, reassess and, if the curse seems to be needed, then go ahead. You are then doing it from a calm place.

Why should you calm down first? Remember the three times three rule. Whatever you send out will return to you, times three, sometimes even more. This is usually the first thing that slows a witch down. Most of us, at some point, had to find out just how true that rule was, and we came to regret our actions. As we grow and evolve, we discover that cursing someone else takes energy that is best spent on more important things. A self-empowered witch has learned that hate and anger take so much energy away from love and joy that it just is not worth it.

Do we just take the crap other people send our way? No, of course not. There are several spell types that you can use in these cases. First, of course, are protection spells. There are hundreds of them, and they can be simple or complicated. One way is to bring up a protective circle just with thought and carry it with you. You can create an amulet of protection and keep it on you at all times. Bless a piece of jewelry that you wear a lot. My favorite way of doing that is to invest the piece with my power so that it deflects any harmful intent sent my way.

Another spell that can be used as a form of protection is a banishing and blessing spell. This is best done when you are not in the heat of the moment and really just want someone to leave you alone. The essence of the spell is to send positive energy to someone, but positive in another place so that they not only leave you alone but go away as well. The heart of the spell is that they go away because something good has happened to them and they are taken away to a better life, far away from you.

You can also use mirror spells to send someone else's negative stuff right back at them. I particularly enjoy this method because you aren't doing something to the person but rather forcing them to deal with their own stuff. Be careful with this one though, do not send any of your own garbage at them, just reflect theirs back to them.

One of Wicca's great lessons is that we are responsible for everything that happens to us, so be careful when assessing what is happening to you. If you have been truly wronged, try first sending their own energy back by using the three times three rule. Accept your own responsibility for whatever happened and make amends on your part. Then just make sure the deities are paying attention and that the other person has to deal with their cosmic debt load. If you are clear in your heart, do it in Perfect Love and Perfect Trust and ask that the other person learn and grow from their experience. Taking responsibility for all our actions also means that we are prepared to stand behind our decisions without fear or regret.

Whether it is to banish or find love, spells are a basic part of the witch's handbook. It is what we do to change ourselves and the world around us. We have accepted that we have the power to alter reality and the spell is the how we do that. Some spells are long-lasting; some spells are instantaneous, but they all work, if you believe that it can work.

Chapter Six

AS YOUR POWER GROWS

Formal modern Wicca as it was originally conceived and practiced is a mystery religion. This where it differs from other forms of witchcraft or folk magic, which are often handed down through generations and are not tied to any religion. Modern Wicca, however, is a religion that employs the tools and practices of witchcraft.

There are two aspects to the practice of a mystery religion, open and closed aspects. The celebration of the seasons and the moon in its cycles do not belong to Wicca or any religion. For that reason, many rites have a celebratory aspect to them, an open aspect often with invitations. Many people will decide that they wish to celebrate, but do not wish to become part of the priesthood of Wicca. Those folks are celebrants. Often, they are also witches who practice magick. There should be no judgment about the religious choices anyone makes as to where they stand in practice.

The closed aspect of Wicca is its initiatory path. Some people decide that they wish to pursue personal growth with the idea that they will become part of the Wiccan priesthood. Those people have chosen to walk the path of the initiate and they become part of the inner circle of people who work with us. On the initiate path, a teacher is required, and the student takes oaths at each stage of initiation to demonstrate that they wish to continue. The journey is not for everyone. Some will walk it awhile then decide they wish to return to the celebrant path. That is great because they have made conscious, intentional decisions about who they are and what they are becoming. In fact, those two questions dominate the initiate path: "Who am I?" becomes "I am becoming." It is a revelation from inside yourself and one that demands a lot of your strength, courage, and dedication.

Wiccan initiations are designed to do two things. First, they recognize that a level of awareness of your power has been achieved. Second, they prepare the way for the next step. They are never simply rewards for good little witches. Working to empower yourself is the heartbeat of being aware of your inner power. That does not mean that you simply know you have the power to cast a spell. It means that you have fully accepted the responsibility for that power. You understand that magick begins within you and that you have begun to focus most of your spellwork on yourself so that you evolve. Instead of always trying to change the world, you are now changing yourself so that your very presence affects the reality around you.

Initiatory Wiccan degrees are not designed solely to award a mastery of a certain amount of data. To see an initiation as a goal to be won is not the proper attitude. To receive the first and second degrees, the teacher decides whether you are ready. Interestingly, for the third degree and elder level, the student makes the initial move because at that level you are being tested to see if you can read your own energy properly. Of course, if you want a formal ritual to be performed, an elder priest or priestess has to be asked, and if they do not think you are truly ready, then it will not happen at that time.

An important note, if you wish to begin on this path, always be very wary of a teacher who will grant you any type of rite of passage for money, or just because you asked. None of these initiatory rites should take place unless you are truly ready, and someone capable of passing the energy on to you will not do it for the wrong reasons.

Wiccans who are working as solitaires have a slightly different journey through degree work. I started as a solitaire simply because there was no one else with whom to work. Many people do the same. Some folks choose to stay solitaires for a variety of reasons. Many, like me, go back and forth through the years. The degree system as outlined below works the same except as a solitaire you decide where you are in the system. If it is important to you that others recognize at what level of degree you stand, then you should consider why that is important to you. The degrees are statements about your level of self-empowerment. The more self-empowered you are, the less other people's opinions matter.

What are the degrees available? That often depends on what path you are following, but the energy is about the same in terms of what elders and teachers are looking for in the student before granting the degree. What follows is a list of the most common degrees granted in modern Wicca.

Dedicant

You have looked and searched and found many spiritual paths, just not the one that is right for you. Wicca speaks to you. You think it might fill that empty place inside with its Goddess and God, and its many ways to express who you are. It allows you to be your own priest or priestess and demands that you accept responsibility for your actions. You find a teacher and begin formal instruction.

Where are you now? What level do you start at and what will you be expected to learn now? This is the stage of the dedicant.

Traditionally, the dedicant stage is a year and a day, although that can be changed by student, teacher, or circumstances. Most teachers will enforce the year and a day, but sometimes things go a bit longer until the first degree is granted. During that year and a day, you will be expected to learn the basics of the Wiccan belief system. It is during this year and a day that you will be introduced to the tools of Wicca and how to use those tools for self-empowerment and celebration.

Other things that come up during this period are your internal energy blocks and how you deal with them. How willing you are to shed your weaknesses, self-deceptions, and fears to discover your greater power and your connection with the cosmos? How connected are you to the earth's energies, herbs, animals, seasons, moon, sun, and stars? Are you willing to walk the path of personal power and stop blaming others for your misfortunes?

All these things sound easy, but they do take courage. The time of the dedicant is not about making corrections; that comes later. This is the time to identify these things so you will know where the work needs to start in order to evolve into your highest self. If you are still walking the Wiccan path a year later, after having started to identify what needs to change inside yourself, then your teacher will pass you and you can prepare for the first degree rites.

Working as a solitaire without benefit of a teacher does not really change what you do during this initial step in embracing Wicca. Even without a teacher, you can learn the basics through books and even online classes. Access to all that information is widely available.

First Degree

A year and a day have passed and you have proved to yourself and your teacher that your commitment is real. You have looked inside yourself and seen your power and begun to accept it and the responsibility that goes with it. You know the basics of Wicca and you have become proficient at raising energy, knowing god forms, sharing energy within a circle, and you have even learned some of the many magickal correspondences. Your first sabbat as priest or priestess was a success, at least no one died, became obsessed, or is babbling in a corner somewhere. Finally, your teacher utters the longed-for words: "Plan your name quest."

The first degree actually takes place in three steps once your teacher has okayed you. The first step is the name quest in which you will go into a meditation to discover your magickal name. A second step is the oral examination. First degree members and above will ask you questions to determine whether you have a knowledge and basic understanding of the basics of Wicca. The third step is the actual ritual where the circle or coven gathers to confer the degree. Provided you pass the first two parts, you can plan the big event, the first degree ritual. The candidate is often in charge of planning for the ritual. After all, it is about them. Solitaires should also plan a rite of their own. The basics of the first degree rite can be found in some books and online. Nothing can make you feel more empowered than standing inside your own circle in front of the cosmos and stating what you have learned about yourself and your own power.

Traditionally, for the ritual itself the candidate goes skyclad, meaning naked, but white or sackcloth and ashes are appropriate. Skyclad was common in the past, but you see it less now. This represents humility and purity of intent. The ritual is a community event, the welcoming of another witch to the secrets of the Wiccan pathway. Solitaires can invite others to witness the rite, especially if the others are walking a solitaire's path, or are friendly to the journey the candidate is making.

After the ritual a party is appropriate. This party is open to any at the discretion of the coven members or solitaire. Everyone should be in a celebratory mood, because first degree rituals are about the joy of defining a spiritual path and taking a real, and assertive step toward self-empowerment. I cannot think of anything else more worthy of celebration than seeing someone step forward and say, "This is who I am and who I am becoming."

There is one final thing that will happen during the first degree rite and that step will take place roughly one lunar cycle after the rite itself. This period of time will give you a chance to settle down from the energy surge of the rite and allow you to think. Then, you will be asked a very important question regarding your journey and your relationship with the coven. "Do you wish to continue on the Initiate's Path?" You have just spent over a year studying Wicca and, by now, you know that after the first degree the really tough internal work begins.

You should consider the posed question very seriously. If you choose to continue, then in many covens you will be asked to reaffirm your binding to your teacher and to its members. The binding that took place at the start of the dedicant phase was only for the year and a day training period. This binding goes much deeper and will require an actual oath. The answer to the question will involve a whole lot of trust on your part if you choose to continue, so carefully consider your answer. At the first degree rite, you were most likely measured with a cord. If you stay, this is the point where that measurement is counted and placed in the keeping of the High Priestess or High Priest. Solitaires should also consider this question as well. No one is holding a measuring cord that represents you, but the cosmos is watching. Take your own measure and commit to your higher self that you intend to hold yourself accountable to your oath.

Sojourns

Sometime during the journey between first degree and second degree a person on the initiate path may be required to make a sojourn. This sojourn will most likely be the first formal trip with the teacher, but not the last. What is a sojourn? These are just a few words about the goals of a sojourn.

A sojourn is really a test of the student. The point of the sojourn is to get the student and teacher into a small space, removed from all the comforts that the student usually hides behind so that the student can evolve into a higher state of being. This encourages the student to rely on the self and to open up to the guidance of the teacher. It is incredibly helpful to have another student along, one who has already been on sojourn. They assist the teacher and have more expanding experiences of their own. If all goes well, the sojourner finds out things about themself that might have taken months otherwise.

Sojourns can and almost always do take place without any framework. Many of trips you have been on may have turned out to be sojourns; you just never called them that. Remember when you ran out of money, the car broke down, there was no place to sleep for hours, when your own personal resources were tested to the limit and there was no one to call on as a fallback position? You found out what you could accomplish on your own, didn't you? You found some deep inner place of strength and self-reliance that you did not know you had, right? Those are sojourn experiences. Do not underestimate yourself and your own life experiences.

Learn the lesson that the cosmos has provided and put it to work in your life.

Second Degree

Working from first degree to second degree is a tough road. It is the time when many things that were fun cease to be fun for a while. It is the journey that questions your spiritual intent and what path will most encourage your personal growth. A witch receives a second degree because they have begun to walk a dark and dangerous path—the internal journey that reveals the truth about who and what they really are. It takes courage to even begin this journey, and it is most often the point where a witch's courage fails and they decide to move to another pathway. Not too hard to understand. The most difficult thing in life to face is our own inner pains, fears, doubts, insecurities, and the memories of how those things came into being. The second degree path working is about learning how to turn those weaknesses into strengths.

Someone is ready for second degree when they realize that they have turned their weaknesses into self-destructive habits, and they have accepted that the very same dark places can be turned into strengths. They have accepted that they have self-deceits that need to be corrected to self-truths so they can more thoroughly reach their power and connection with the cosmos. It does not mean that they have learned how to do that yet, just that they know they can, and should in order to be more aware and powerful in their own reality. Just as in the move from dedicant to first degree, before you can take your second degree you will be faced with an oral examination performed by second degrees and above. This examination is different because you will not be asked too many questions about facts and figures, but rather about your personal emotional addictions, and how you feed them.

Second degree is not about learning the dark side of the craft, but rather it is about using your inner darkness to achieve a higher purpose. You will spend much time working with your shadow self. If all goes well, your power will grow as you embrace those dark parts of yourself and learn how to use that strength. The walking of the second degree path prepares you for the leaps of faith that the third degree demands. You are not ready for that next degree until you are ready to let go of those emotional addictions. That journey can take a long time to achieve, so do not expect to spend just a year and day working through the second degree. It can take a few extra months or even years depending on the person.

Solitaires can also do this dark internal work. Turn to trusted friends or mentors for assistance. Ask for their thoughts on what you use as places to hide from yourself. This is an excellent time to call on the elementals and the four elements to assist in uncovering the dark places within yourself. Consider a twenty-four-hour solar drawing down that can light up your darker self as described in Chapter Five. Do not be afraid to seek professional counseling if you cannot find your way to the light after working with your shadow self. Asking for help and guidance is a big step in self-empowerment to ask for and accept guidance when you need it.

The second degree rite itself is closed to all except those at that level or higher. This is due to the nature of the ritual itself. A first degree initiation is about the candidate, their commitment to the path and to the coven, as well as the group's commitment to the candidate. That rite is a community event. However, the second degree rite is much more personal. It is not about community, but about the initiate's inner journey. Darkness is often pulled in by the priest and priestess and revealed to all present. All attendees must be ready for the experience so that it does not damage them. The candidate's own darkness is also laid bare for all to see. That is not something that just everyone is ready to share, hence the rite is closed. The after party, however, is open to all. The more the merrier as a matter of fact because the ritual participants may be in a pretty strange place. It helps to have others around to get everyone grounded. If you get the chance to attend a second degree celebration party, do so. Be part of someone else's journey; it can only strengthen your own.

Third Degree

It is at this stage of the degree journey that solitaires and those who work with a group have the most in common. The journey through third degree is the constant juxtaposition of alone versus community. It is during this journey that you must learn how to be an independent individual and yet share yourself completely with others. Those emotional addictions rear their head again, but now you will not use others to feed your addictions; and you would rather be alone than continue a life that is dictated by your personal melodrama. You are ready for your third degree when you realize that no one has any power over you if you do not let them, and you have begun to live that way. You no longer buy into the reality of others, or at least you catch yourself quickly when you do. You accept full responsibility for your actions and blaming others usually does not even occur to you, or at least when you try to shift blame, you always come back to yourself.

Third degree rites are usually closed rites. Few of these rituals are ever performed publicly. That is for two reasons: someone actually reaching a third degree is pretty rare and third is the most personal and internal. Of the degrees it is the only one that the initiate actually performs themself. In group settings, the high priest and high priestess are there just for fun. No one need attend. No one has to be there at all. This rite is between the initiate and the cosmos. There is no need for witnesses unless they just want to be there and the initiate wants them there. Normally the rite is attended by third degrees and beyond. Other witnesses sometimes stand outside of the circle. Those standing outside will see and hear only what they are able to understand at their stage of development.

If the other third degrees and elders in your magickal community sense you are ready for this step, they will support your initiation to third degree. You are not required to have a formal rite, but if you wish to have one, brace yourself. There will be another oral examination. As with second degree, the questions will not have anything to do with information. Rather, these questions will be about your plans for your magickal growth: What will you do next? There is a reason that most magickal groups are light on third degree initiates. Most witches who achieve third degrees are out forming their own groups, hiving off their old coven to start new things.

Solitaires have been working alone for a long time by this point. Through their interactions with the world around them they have reached a deep level of understanding their personal power and the responsibility that goes with that power. Both they and third degree witches in a group have learned true acceptance of self and others. These witches are not perfect; they have just learned that there is still so much to learn. They have also learned how to read the patterns around themselves and see that they are the center of the matrix. Third degree witches know that the only really important spell you cast in your life is the one that creates you and that it is constant and ongoing, conscious, and subconscious. When the third degree initiate fully embraces joy and peace over melodrama, it is time to consider the role of elder.

Elder

The day has come when you realize you are tired. You enjoy the celebrations and workings of magick. You just no longer want to be at the center of those activities. If you have worked with a group, you can hand over your wand to someone who is ready for it and sit down. If you have been working as a solitaire you just realize one day that it has been a while since you cast a formal circle, yet your magick is always working. You are now moving into the elder stage.

Are elders completely self-empowered? Usually not, but they have reached a place in life where self-empowerment is a regular and ongoing process. They have learned that they are truly unique. They know that their powers are not available to just everyone and that they have a responsibility to live as much as possible within those powers. Most elders are solitaires by choice. They have learned that being unique means lots of loneliness and they are okay with that. Being special does not make you more important, just more responsible.

True elders will care intensely that you reach your own true power but will not pontificate to you about how best to do that. They enjoy being liked by others but are not willing to sacrifice who they are to make that happen. They laugh when someone does not "get it" and never let anyone else's opinion upset their personal reality. Elders speak the truth but are also aware that the truth hurts and is not acceptable to others.

It all sounds simple, like stuff you already know, and it is, in theory. It is the getting there that takes a lot of energy and time and patience. Knowing it is one thing, living it is something else again, and elders live it.

There are formal eldering ceremonies, but they do not happen often. That is normally because there are not enough elders around to perform the rite. They typically take place at extremely large gatherings where several groups have come together for another celebration. My own was simple. We had two elders who worked with us. After rites they sat at their special table and enjoyed the party. One day they called me over to join them. That was it. Another time a solitaire had joined our rite for the evening. Afterward, he was called to join us at that table. It was a recognition of his stage in the degree system. If you have been invited to a formal eldering ceremony, do not hesitate to accept. They do not happen often.

If reaching the elder stage is your goal, you are not there yet. Elders, true elders, are the rarest of things. You will see many claim or be given an elder title because of their advanced knowledge and use of the tools of magick, but not because they have reached the true energy of the Elder. Few are able to make all the internal corrections necessary to be able to live within their power most of the time. Few are able to accept their own rarity, uniqueness, and specialness to be an elder of any path. If you know someone who has, you are lucky.

High Priest and High Priestess

It is common in modern formal Wicca for people to start taking on students of their own during their journey through second degree. By the time they are thinking about taking that third degree initiation odds are they are already running their own coven or about to do so. Anyone who is called a High Priest or High Priestess is a third degree.

In Wicca we honor everyone as their own priestess or their own priest but being a High Priestess or High Priest is different.

Because I have worked with teaching circles, I was able to see close up the differences as people worked to become what they imagined was the penultimate goal—becoming a High Priestess or a High Priest. The final thing a dedicant had to do to reach first degree was to host a sabbat as the priestess or priest. It was during that process that many began to understand that the role of being a high anything was not what it seemed. When you stand at the center of the circle you must be open to whatever energies are present. Those energies include that of deities and the people who are part of the rite.

When you are a High Priestess or a High Priest, your responsibility does not end there. You are responsible for the circle members all the time. To truly fulfill your role as a bringer of godhead to the people with whom you share magickal work, you must always be available to the members and to any deity who wishes to interact with the circle. It is hard and exhausting. If a student fully understood that after they held their first sabbat, I knew they had it in them to run their own circle when they were ready to do so.

This is a place where solitaires really shine. They have always been their own priest or priestess. If their journey has been one of self-empowerment, then they have reached a gnosis of the deity within and the deity without. Their connection to the elements of the circle is strong and clean. When they choose to join a group for some event, they normally have no trouble sharing energy with everyone present. Their solitary rites, be they celebrations or working circles, usually resonate in the cosmos with great power because their connections to all the energies is so strong. They have empowered themselves right from the start to be their own High Priest and High Priestess.

Student/Teacher Relationships

One of the surest ways to grow and constantly be in search of one's internal power is to have a one-on-one teacher. That can be a great advantage because the teacher's job is not to tell you what to do or how to live your life, but to assist you in finding your true will and following that will. Even third degrees and elders benefit from having teachers because we always need someone around to point out when we are not being true to our magick. Sometimes a teacher appears for a brief time to assist with something specific. When that lesson is learned, that teacher moves on to other things.

It was once a tradition for the student to become an apprentice to the teacher and live with them for a time in order to learn at the teacher's feet. You still see this today in the world of learning trades such as electricity or carpentry. The student starts as an apprentice then advances to journeyman status. Ultimately, they become the expert and take on apprentices of their own.

The days of this type of apprentice relationship in the magickal teaching system have mostly passed, although from personal experience I can tell you that many students have spent much time following me around and learning a great deal just by watching me live my life. To a certain degree they learned more when I myself made a mistake and had to correct for it. They learned, if nothing else, that I too am not perfect and am still growing. This is also a valuable lesson.

Keep in mind that if a teacher is not honest or correct in the tools and lessons they have provided, the backlash can be tremendous. The teacher also runs the risk of receiving backlash if the student misuses information, or if the student does something wrong because the teacher has never taught that lesson or taught it properly. With that responsibility, what does the teacher get in return? One great advantage to the teacher is that nothing teaches us like teaching someone else. You are constantly looking for a better way to communicate the lesson. That deepens your knowledge of the lesson.

Money is not a good payment. Let's face it; there is no way to financially charge for something that is available 24/7 once the teacher says yes.

The truest payment is service to the teacher. Service can take many forms from mowing the grass to making sure the teacher has a plate of food at a gathering. Most service should be student generated. It can be very revealing of the student how they choose to perform service. If it is something they want to do for the teacher, then it comes from the heart and has no grudge involved in it. It can also be very revealing to see who has trouble performing service, and not "being able to figure out what they need me to do" is a way of avoiding service.

Some teachers have a hard time accepting service because they wish to remain independent of the student. As in all things, a great gift is also a great burden. Being unable to accept service can do the student a great disservice. Many of them will never learn to honor their teachers, and in not honoring the teacher, they do not really know how to honor themselves. Aside from that, not accepting service sends a subtle message that the lessons and time of the teacher have no value.

An Important Warning

One warning about service: if a teacher demands money or sex in return for lessons, then take a moment to re-examine the options. The student-teacher relationship can often be abused. In terms of money, if the student offers money in payment of lessons, that student may simply be someone who believes that paying for something can make sure it happens. Paying in money usually means that the student can dictate the terms of the teaching, and for some students and teachers that is more comfortable.

Where sex is concerned, that is a time-honored abuse of power. If sex becomes part of the relationship, it must be consensual and never a payment for lessons in magick. If at any point the student feels that they must have sex with the teacher in order to continue the student/teacher relationship, then the sex is not truly consensual. One of the greatest moments of self-empowerment is the moment you can say no to someone who is demanding sex. No relationship is worth giving into such an order. Better to walk away, or even run away, than be abused sexually. Find a new teacher.

If a strong emotional and sexual bond does naturally and con- sensually develop between the student and the teacher, especially if the relationship takes a serious turn toward a long-term commit- ment, then it is probably best if the student takes another teacher. The conflict of interest is too great. There is a reason why doc- tors are not encouraged to treat their own families and the same rules apply here. Sometimes the teacher has a vested interest, even subconsciously, in keeping someone where they are instead of that student taking their power.

Solitaires and Teachers

Walking the path alone and not taking a teacher has it owns chal- lenges and rewards. You will have to seek out the lessons you need. As you begin there is a lot of information available to you through books and the internet. It will be up to you to pick through all that stuff. An early step in finding your power is to determine what you want and need, and to leave the other stuff alone. That decision by itself empowers you. As your journey continues you will find less work available in a written format. You will have to seek out the works that you need to guide you. Some of those works will be of a magickal, spiritual nature. Other works will not seem to have a spiritual aspect to them. It is a huge statement about how deep your self-empowerment goes when you listen to your instincts and just know that what you need at this step in your journey may best be found in a history book. The conversation you have with the clerk in the checkout line may well be the lesson you need right now. A solitaire's best teacher is their own instinct. Always pay attention to what those voices inside you are whispering.

Those whispering voices are consistently going to be your best guide. As you progress through the degrees, which is representative of your growing awareness of your power, the voices will get louder. If they say you need a teacher, send a message out to the cosmos. A teacher will appear. If you hear a whisper of, "you need a student." Send that message out. Next thing you know, someone will be asking for some lessons.

Take the next step in your power by listening to the voices of your own instinct.

Chapter Seven
LIFE PASSAGES

From birth to death the human experience is filled with moments of moving from one stage of life to another. In our modern world many of those moments have lost a lot of their power. While we do celebrate birth, graduation, marriage, and other major achievements, and we certainly go into great mourning at death, we often avoid, or just do not acknowledge some of the more subtle passages of life. The moments that we ignore are often the most important moments, like a young girl's first menses or a young boy at the minute he starts reaching for manhood. It is those times, subtle though they may be, that are the signal that a new phase of life is approaching, and the person needs more than just a celebration. They need guidance and encouragement to reach that new phase with as much personal power as they can find.

Life stages and how they are represented in Wicca are just as important. In my tradition, we teach that the God divides His life into Godling, Warrior/Provider, and Sage. The Goddess is Maiden, Mother, Crone. These represent the stages of life that we all go through. But it is even more complex than that. Early stages evolve into more mature and developed stages as we grow and achieve our goals. A child learns to walk and talk. Then the child starts school. These are moments of growth that should be celebrated. As we move through our teens and early adulthood we learn to drive, buy a car, register to vote, go on a first date. All are steps toward our growing power and awareness of that power.

As Wiccans we celebrate all the phases of life, even when death takes someone to the Summerlands, we mourn, but we also celebrate that person's life and their choice to move to another phase of the soul's evolution. We do consider these rites to be sabbats, as well as the Blessing of the Animals that we do in the autumn. The Rites of Passage that we celebrate are listed below along with short descriptions. These rites are fitted to group work, but for solitaires they can be adapted in whatever you wish. In fact, adapting a rite to meet your specific needs empowers you even more as you transition through the stages. You are willingly accepting that you aged. The rites indicate that you are ready to move into the knowledge and power of the next stage.

Belly Blessing

Even before a new life is brought into the world, we acknowledge that a life is present. A group of women, usually in the mother stage or older, gather together with the pregnant woman and bless both her and her unborn child for the Belly Blessing ritual. This is done in the hope that the birth will go easy for both mother and child, and that they both experience protection and love from the beginning.

How to Celebrate

It is the choice of the birthing mother to decide who attends the blessing. Traditionally only women attended this rite, and the men conducted a rite for the father. Today the mother is free to make the choice with which she is most comfortable. What does have to be there is a cord that is tied around the pregnant woman, either her wrist or waist. Each person present must contribute a piece of string to this cord. The pregnant woman should wear the cord until the safe delivery of her child. In some celebrations, each guest also has a piece of cord. If that is the case, they should keep theirs on until that time as well.

Correspondences and Associations

Artemis was the Goddess of birthing mothers and one of Her sacred stones is jasper. For this rite use green and red jasper to bless the unborn and the mother, during the rite itself. It is entirely appropriate to give those objects to the mother as a gift for her and the coming child.

Timing

There are no strict rules on when to do this rite. It would be good to do it in the third trimester as the birth is approaching. If possible, the period of the waxing moon in its second quarter before it is actually full would be appropriate. Monday is the moon's day, so a Monday is a good day. However, in our world today it is not always easy to get together on a Monday, either day or night. Friday, because it is Venus's day, works as well. Sunday is also a good day. It is the day of Sol, a masculine deity, but it is a day of blessing, too.

Birthing

This rite is not to be confused with the Wiccaning. This rite is celebrated at the moment of birth, usually by a High Priestess with the High Priest standing close to give protection. The rite is designed to welcome the new soul to the physical world and to give thanks to all deities who aided in the birth and kept both mother and child protected and safe. The best part of this celebration is that the baby will, hopefully, be surrounded by warmth and love and hear only positive things at the time of birth, starting her or him out with a personal power jolt of self-confidence.

It would be wrong not to mention that it is always wise to have clergy, of whatever religion, very close during a birth, just in case they are needed. If you are following the Wiccan path and there are problems at birth, the presence of clergy will not make your sorrow go away, but they can make sure that certain procedures are followed if the worst should occur.

How to Celebrate

If at all possible, the High Priestess should be present at the birth, and the High Priest either there, or nearby. Once the baby is safely into this world, the High Priestess and High Priest should have on hand a small representation of the four elements, and each should be presented to the new life and to the parents. The breath of life should be blown into the baby's face, gently. In the past this was done by the opposite gender Priest or Priestess, but today it can be either gender. Always go with what makes you most comfortable.

Correspondences and Associations

Juno/Hera from the Greco/Roman pantheon is a goddess who protects children. You can call on Her to bless both the newborn child and the mother. One of her best-known symbols is the peacock. Bring one, or something similar, and wave it over the new child and the mother calling in the protection of this goddess.

Timing

The timing of the birthing blessing is almost completely dictated by that baby. If you can be present at the birth, then that is the time to do the blessing. Beyond that, as soon after the birth as possible.

Wiccaning/Naming

Giving a new child a name is very important because that is how they will face the world and define themselves until they come into their own power and take names that reflect their power. As part of Western culture the name that the parents give a child is the name that will dominate their life. The rite that most people are familiar with that is similar to this one is christening. A Wiccaning serves pretty much the same purpose. A Wiccaning should occur as soon after birth as possible, but definitely within the first year. It is at this rite that the new life is presented to the coven and the given name is pronounced to everyone. There is usually a God Father and a Goddess Mother to take charge of the child's religious upbringing, or to agree in open circle that they will make sure that this child will always be allowed to follow his or her own true will. During the rite, all four quarters as well as the Mother and Father of us all are formally called upon to bless and gift the child.

As in the birthing ceremony this rite is not intended to push the child onto the Wiccan path, but to introduce the child to the coven, and the cosmos by a given name and to let all know that the child is protected in this new life as it starts the journey through childhood.

How to Celebrate

This rite should be as public as the parents wish and include as much of the child's family as can possibly attend. The parents will choose the God and Goddess parents and it is those four who will present the child to the High Priest and High Priestess at the altar. At that presentation the High Priest and High Priestess ask the child's name and present the child to the coven. The name of the child can be either the legal name or if the parents wish a Wiccan name. The God and Goddess parents will be asked to take an oath to protect the child's right to pursue its true will. Then the child should be presented to the coven as a whole to receive the circle's commitment to assist the child in its walk through life. Once that is done, the child should be presented to each quarter for the blessings of that particular element. Then the child should be presented at the altar to receive the blessings of the God and Goddess.

Correspondences and Associations

Most groups or solitaires have a pantheon with which they work most comfortably. Invoke the mother and father of that pantheon to bless the child. If you are performing the rite for someone outside of your group or have been asked to do so as a solitaire, use the deity structure of the pantheon with which the parents are most comfortable. If they have no pantheon, stick with your own.

Whether you have people standing at each quarter or you are doing the quarter blessings yourself, bless the child with some small representation of each element.

Timing

This rite should be done within the first year after birth; as close to the birth as possible. You are introducing the child to the cosmos and saying its name out loud. This is not a secret event to be hidden in darkness. The best time of day is under the bright sun of noon, or in the hours around that time. Aim for a time when the moon is full, or close to full. Avoid a period of moon void-of-course.

It is almost impossible to avoid all planetary retrogrades, but definitely avoid Mercury, Venus, and Mars retrogrades. If you, or someone involved, can do the astrology, aim for a period when the ruling planet of the child's astrological sign is in a prominent position. That is not necessary, but it can't hurt.

Adopting a Child

The three previous rites are aimed at parents who physically birth a child, but adopting a child is also a huge blessing and deserves to be celebrated. All of those rites can be easily adapted for families with adopted children of any age. You can also use your power as the prospective parent or parents to hasten and ease this journey as the adoption process is long and arduous. Consider these following workings as way to adapt the rites and cast a spell to make the adoption successful.

Application Blessing

Instead of a belly blessing, you will bless the adoption application. After you fill the papers out but before you turn them in, hold a rite with you and whomever else is involved in the process: your partner, siblings, grandparents, aunts, uncles, cousins, family, and friends. During this rite, you will ask for the adoption request to be approved, instead of asking for an easy birth. Then perform the same cord ritual as in the belly blessing. Since you can't tie it around the papers, place it in a space that is dedicated to the adoption. If you have a statue or painting of a pregnant woman, that is perfect. Each person present must contribute a piece of string to this cord.

Leave the cord there until that new member of the family is safely home with you. As with the belly blessing, if each person present also has a piece of the cord, then they should keep theirs on until that time as well. You can also call upon Artemis, the Goddess of birthing mothers and the protection of children, to open and guide the path between that child and your family. Use green and red jasper to bless the adoption.

Meeting the Child

If you are present at the birthing, then just follow the same rite that is spelled out above. If you are not present at the birth but find out via a phone call that a child is ready for you, adapt the birthing ritual to meet that moment. The rite should welcome the new child to your family and give thanks to all deities upon whom you called who aided in making the adoption happen. Ask to keep the child protected and safe and bring them safely to your home. This is the time to ask for the adoption to be finalized. It can take up to a year for the adoption to be finalized in the legal system and the judge to sign the final papers.

Adoption Celebration

If you have adopted an infant, then the Wiccaning rite is the same. If the child is older and already has a name, then you won't do the rite the same way. Instead of a first name, the name you are giving this child is your surname. That critical court date is the timing for this naming celebration. When the adoption is final and the child is legally a member of your family, you will celebrate with a rite.

This rite should be as public as the parents wish and include as much of the child's family as can possibly attend. The parents will choose the God and Goddess parents and it is those four who will present the child to the High Priest and High Priestess at the altar. At that presentation the High Priest and High Priestess will ask the child's name. Loudly announce the now legal surname of this member of the family. After that the Wiccaning rite should follow the same steps as the one above.

Entering Adulthood

Wiccans recognize childhood as its own life stage and not some diluted adulthood. As the child grows, the next significant rites of life are performed as the child leaves childhood behind and enters the age of accountability.

It is important that the elders and parents take into account the maturity level of the child so that the ceremonies are performed at the right time. Emotional and mental maturity are just as important as physical maturity. Some children are mentally ready when their bodies mature, some are not. Take into account both the body and the emotional maturity of the child before planning a rite. Then this new life stage can be recognized with these rituals.

Maiden/Godling Rite

This is the moment that a child starts reaching for adulthood. The onset of menses is the clear sign for girls. It can be a bit harder for boys, but there are indications during the early to middle teen years that a boy is starting to reach for manhood, such as facial hair and voice change. Do the signs indicate that the person is an adult and should be expected to act like one? Not in twenty-first century America. We tend to have a prolonged adolescence. We do not reach our legal majority until we're eighteen and many things are off limits until the age of twenty-one. We usually live with our parents until we finish high school and often stay on their health insurance and are counted as tax deductions until we finish college. However, entering the teens is a critical time in the young person's life. They are reaching past their parents and families to begin looking ahead.

The following two rites are designed to help a young person begin their path of personal empowerment, to give them confidence in themselves, and to show that they are surrounded by folks other than blood family who will assist and guide them. The greatest gift parents can give a child at this point of life is freedom. Not the freedom to run around like an idiot, but the freedom to reach past the nuclear family and find new role models. My parents gave me that gift. I joined clubs that assisted in the development of young adults. Those clubs were led by adults who became different role models for me.

The secret my parents did not tell me and I learned many years later was that they could monitor what was happening through those adults. As I matured through my own mother stage of life, I became that type of adult for many young people. I was trusted by teens to guard the secrets of their youth, and I was trusted by the parents to always let them know if the child was in actual danger. It was only as I was filling that role that I began to understand what my parents had done for me and what a tremendous gift it was.

Historically, the rites that introduce the young person into this stage of life have been gender specific and I will share them as originally designed. However, attitudes are changing in our world today regarding gender. Parents can make different choices about how every gender is represented in the rites. The most important voice in that decision, however, is the young person for whom the rite is being conducted. Allow that person to begin their journey to self-empowerment by deciding how gender is reflected in their rite.

During the rite, the maiden Goddess or the young Godling is pulled down into the teen so that they can begin to feel the power of the cosmos as an adult feels that power. They are not yet ready to become adults, but these rites are designed to start them out on a path that will take them into adulthood with a strong sense of the responsibility that comes with adulthood.

Godling Rite

At this point in his life, a boy is recognized as a young man by the coven and is ready to begin his journey into adult responsibilities. He is now able to spark a life into creation and he must learn how to use his power responsibly. This is his time to explore the world and learn to know his own skills and abilities, to become an individual, pursuing his own destiny. During this stage the young man will go on many quests, both physical and spiritual. He'll learn to drive, maybe take his first job. He may attend religious services that are different from what he has always known. It is the time for him to try many things and have many adventures. His responsibility to the coven is to learn himself and begin to take responsibility for his actions.

Maidening Rite

Traditionally, the first stage of a woman's life is associated with the maiden and is often recognized by the coven with a Maidening Rite. The girl's body has started menstruation and she is now capable of having a child. That does not mean she should rush out and get pregnant, only that she can and now has a new level of responsibility. Now is the time of life when a young woman discovers her power and her boundaries. She learns to define herself without anyone else, learns how not to be dependent, so later she can learn how to be dependent without sacrificing her own personality. One important note, the term *maiden* in this case does not mean physical virginity: rather, the virginity of spirit and defining one's individuality. This stage is about not losing oneself in the definition anyone else puts on her.

How to Celebrate

The rites themselves are very similar. Traditionally men perform the Godling Rite and women perform the Maidening. However, as I noted, this has changed in recent years as gender definitions broaden. The choice of attendees is up to you. As for the rites themselves, they are often held in secret. During the rite make certain that all four quarters are presented to the new adult with the twist that they should now begin to study those powers from an adult perspective. The same is true for the presentation of the God or Goddess to the new adult.

For the Godling right, the child is taken out into the world of humans for at least a day. This day is dedicated to taking the emerging adult beyond what he or she knows and with which he/she is comfortable. This puts them through test of courage. If rural settings are available, then this is time to take a solitary hike through the forest. You can even take them to a local park for that hike. Urban settings include tests like grocery shopping on his own or taking public transport. Traditionally new maidens were not put into these tests. Their tests came over cook fires and making sure the young children were cared for properly. However, in our modern world, either gender can be tested in either way.

A party should follow each rite with all genders presents. This is a celebration of a new stage of life and the party should reflect that. Having everyone present for the party is an indication that even though the new adult is learning the secrets of their own gender identity, the world is made up of many gender identifications.

Correspondences and Associations

The crescent moon and the rising sun are the most obvious associations to this new adult. Artemis is also a protector of young people. Mercury, or Hermes, is a god associated with youth. During the rite you can use silver and gold colors in candles and clothing and jewelry. Those colors represent the moon and the sun.

The deity structure is very much up to the young person who is being celebrated. Let his or her voice be the loudest on the choices. Not only does that indicate that you have begun to respect their choices, but it puts adult responsibility in their hands.

Timing

The best time to perform the Godling Rite is during the first sliver of the New Moon, the Hunter's Moon. This early moon represents youth, but youth that is growing. The Maidening is best performed during the early phases of the First Quarter Moon because that is the goddess in her maiden aspect. Avoid moon void-of-course and as many planetary retrogrades as possible.

Handfasting

At some point in life many folks will choose a partner with whom to walk. Sometimes this is a permanent arrangement, sometimes it is temporary. Either way, any commitment should be celebrated. This particular rite is called a handfasting in Wicca. How legal and formal the handfasting is depends on what the couple wants. When I was serving the role of High Priestess, I was considered a member of the legal clergy. While filling that role, I would not perform a handfasting, legal or otherwise, without first counseling the couple. Some traditions may require a year and a day of a trial marriage. If at the end of the trial the couple wished to commit more permanently, then a public handfasting can be performed. It is a celebration that the entire coven performs with the couple. Both the couple and the coven recognize that for this time they choose to walk together and learn the lessons of life as a team. The independence of early adulthood is now to become a partnership, a blending of the separate energies into a third energy, the marriage.

It should be noted here that in Wicca there are no rules about who can be handfasted. We will perform handfastings for same sex couples or even groups of more than two who wish to make their life commitment before the public and the gods. The traditional rites can be easily adjusted according to the wishes of those who are taking this steps.

Additionally, while Wiccans do honor the state of marriage and take handfastings very seriously, it is also recognized that life can go its own way. Handfasted couples may find that they no longer can walk together. Handfastings are not done "til death do us part," but usually for as long as "life and love keep us together." If at some point the couple wishes to break their bond and they legally get a divorce, they should also perform a magickal rite called a handparting, during which the cord that bound them as a couple is cut and destroyed, preferably by the same High Priest and High Priestess who handfasted them.

How to Celebrate

The handfasting rite can be as formal or informal as the couple wishes. It can follow the more traditional patterns of a wedding or be very different. Either way, it is the couple's decision. A handfasting does have certain unique elements that are not typical to mainstream weddings. The rite is performed by both a High Priestess and a High Priest so that the God and Goddess are equally represented. The couple should choose sponsors to bring them into the circle. It is our belief that neither party is "given away," but both parties are being presented to the altar. During the course of the rite the couple should be given blessings from the God and the Goddess. Also, the couple should travel to each quarter to receive blessings and commissions from those powers.

There are two items that cannot be left out: the rings and the cord. The rings are blessed by the High Priest and High Priestess just as in a more mainstream ceremony. The other item is the cord, which will be used to bind the couple together. It is the moment when the right hands of the bride and groom are bound that the marriage is performed. Traditionally, the High Priest and High Priestess make the binding cord to be used during the rite.

Another item that is fun, but not necessary, is the broom over which the couple leaps at the end of the rite. For Wiccans this represents that the binding is as permanent as the couple wishes.

Correspondences and Associations

Planning a handfasting is as complicated as planning any wedding. It all begins with whomever is making this commitment. They should choose the deity structure. Once that decision has been made, add the correct correspondences for those deities.

A general suggestion is that whichever pantheon is chosen, choose deities known for faith and love and their ability to make lasting commitments.

Timing

Once again, handfastings are as complicated as weddings. Finding a time that works for everyone is almost impossible. Keep this in mind, the only people who must be there are the ones making the commitment and whoever is performing the rite. It is best to do this one when the moon is full or nearly full. If you choose daytime ceremony, do it when the sun is high in sky. Avoid moon void-of-course and as many planetary retrogrades as possible.

Mother/Father Rites

As a young person, the focus is often selfish and internal, as it should be, but as life moves along there may come a time when others become more important to us than ourselves. The desire to protect others, even at one's own risk; desiring to teach and guide others are both ways that we reach for power outside our own self-definition. Others' definitions are as important to you as your own. This is the next stage of our evolution: the mother or father stage. It is a gross misconception that one must have birthed children to reach this state, but it is sometimes the only way someone stops centering on themselves. Even with the coming of children, some people sadly never really reach outside their own focus to begin to live for others. Regardless of how you achieve this state and make this transition, it is truly a cause for celebration. The Mother and Father rites are designed to celebrate this transition. It is at these rites that the circle celebrates the evolution of someone who is ready to make others more important than themselves.

Fathering

The person is now ready to defend the circle, the coven, the family, whatever external group that is defined as needing this energy. It is during this stage that the person's power takes on a life of its own in how it is expressed it in a public way. This person now extends protection and guidance to others.

The sword and its secrets dominate the Fathering rite, which should be performed by people in the father or older stages of life. They know those secrets and how to wield them.

Mothering

At this stage, the person is entering the stage where caring for others is a priority. The Mother stage also says that the person has accepted there are many others beyond oneself that need to be nurtured. This person focuses on what others are doing as much as what she is doing.

The Mothering Rite is dominated by the cauldron because it is the source of all creation. The rite should be performed by people in the mother or older, stage of life as they know the secrets of the cauldron and how to use them. The secrets are passed on to the person being honored.

How to Celebrate

These rites are similar to the rites of the Godling and Maiden except that they are calling in different aspects of the God and Goddess. This is the time to call upon deities who perform the role of mother and father. The pantheon used is up to the group, or the solitaire, but each pantheon has deities who fill those roles. The High Priest should assist the casting of the Mothering Rite circle and then remove himself. The High Priestess should assist the casting of the Fathering Rite circle and then remove herself. During the ritual, the next level of secrets should be conveyed, which include the sharing of the wisdom of the cauldron and what it means about the Divine Feminine; or the secrets of the sword and what it means about the Divine Masculine.

Correspondences and Associations

The chosen pantheon dictates what the correspondences will be. However, it is fairly consistent that the mother is represented by the full moon and the father is represented by the sun at the height of the day. Gold and silver can be the dominant colors in candles and clothing. It is common in many traditions to use green for mother energies and blue for father energies.

The cauldron and the sword are very prominent features of these two rites, so make sure that those symbols are represented.

Timing

The timing of the Father rite should revolve around the sun, rather than the moon. Sunday is the best day for the fathering rite. The timing of the Mother rite should revolve around the moon, preferably the Full moon. Monday, as the moon's day, is the best day.

Avoid moon void-of-course and as many planetary retrogrades as possible.

Eldering

Toward the end of the life stages of mother and father these people are usually ready to begin the move out of public roles, stepping aside for others to take those responsibilities, and they enter elder roles. This is a time that many people never reach, not because the calendar does not say they are there, but because they never stop needing to have a voice in the world around them. It is the truly evolved souls who realize that the world simply does not always listen to the wisdom and guidance they provide. While their wisdom might be needed more at this stage than at any other time, not everyone wants to slow down and hear it. An elder will step back to see who will actually ask. The elder knows when to speak and when to be silent. Whatever gender designation, usually the coven recognizes them with a special rite. This is often when they step down from the official roles and are ready to let others take the reins of leadership, but they will always be there to assist.

This is a time of great power and a culmination of the external power of the adult. It is not necessarily the point of entering old age, but the point when the power is still used externally many ways, just not as loudly. Elders are the storytellers, and it is in this form that they pass on much of the wisdom they have acquired. The elder role may be called Matron or Crone and Patron or Sage.

Saging

As a Sage, Patron, or Grandfather, the person is no longer responsible for the spark of the circle or family. He is ready to share wisdom, compassion, and strength, but no longer expected to pick up the Sword to protect others. Now the sage can spend his time caring about how the others grow. His spark is now the spark of wisdom.

Croning

The Crone, Matron, or Grandmother is no longer standing at the center of the circle or the family. Women in the mother role are now taking care of those responsibilities. It is now her time to teach younger folks how to laugh at life without fear, how to face death with respect, and how to age with grace. Her center is now one of grace.

How to Celebrate

The other rites that have traditionally celebrated gendered specific stages of life have a secretive aspect to them. The rites that celebrate eldering do not. The secrets have already been passed or will be in intimate talks and inner journeys. Other elders typically perform the ritual, because the energy must be from them to the new elder, but everyone can join in the rite and celebration. For both the new crone and the new sage this is time of joy and the start of preparations for the journey into the Summerlands to rest and form the next life.

Since this rite is public and the genders are not separated for it, it can be as formal as the new elder and other elders desire. If the decision is to perform a formal rite to acknowledge that a person has moved into a new stage, then it can be performed by the entire circle. In fact, the younger members can hold the quarters. The priest and priestess should be in the mother and father stage. Other elders can hold roles if they like, but it is often more appropriate for them to sit in the northern sector of the circle. The new elder should be presented to them first before being introduced to everyone present.

Entering the elder role in life is not quite the same as being recognized as an elder in magickal groups. Magickal elders are held in great regard because of their spiritual journey. Life elders are those people we turn to for advice and guidance and comfort when life throws us curve balls. We all know people who are life elders; grandparents are the best example.

Correspondences and Associations

Once again, the chosen pantheon dictates what the correspondences will be. The waning moon is a correspondence to the crone. The sage is best represented by the sun as it begins to move toward setting in the western sky. Gold and silver can be the dominant colors in candles and clothing. It is also appropriate to use black, gray, or even white because they are the colors we associate with aging.

Timing

Saging rites should take place as the sun begins to set. Sunday is the best day, but Wednesday works, too. This is especially true if the pantheon is Nordic because Odin was usually depicted as a grandfather energy. The timing of the rite should revolve around the sun as it gets lower in the western sky. The timing of the Crone rite should revolve around the waning moon. Not the night of the new moon, but a few days before that aspect. Monday always works for the moon.

Death

When the time has come to end this life cycle and take a break, a death rite is performed to recognize that passing and that soon they will return to the Wheel of Life to begin again. This rite often assists in preparing the way for that return. This rite also assists those of us left behind in our mourning process. It is time to say goodbye to a person of power and celebrate with joy having known them.

As with all living things on the Wheel of Life, humans die, too. Not only do humans die, but beloved pets and familiars pass to the next phase of their soul's evolution as well. Being Wiccan does not stop death, nor does it stop the pain of losing someone, human or animal, that you love. There is no way that those of us left behind do not grieve and mourn, because we miss their physical presence. However, in Wicca, we also celebrate the passing. Funerary rites are a celebration of the life and lessons taught by the person who has passed and what one hopes was a well-lived life. If the deceased was an animal, then not much is different.

Such rites can be performed at the burial site or with the scattering of ashes or at a memorial service. In other words, in all the ways the other religions do this. The decision can be complicated when the person who has died has left no provisions as to how to perform the rites and their funeral comes under the auspices of non-Wiccan family members. Then it becomes critical that the Wiccan family of that person perform a memorial service to send this soul on its way into the Summerlands and the next incarnation.

If the loved one who has passed is not Wiccan, yet there is a Wiccan who is in deep mourning over the loss, the witch or coven can surround the person who is in mourning with our love and support and perform a rite of passing to ease the deceased's passage and the pain of the living. In any and all of these rites it is important to remember that grief is real and life is for the living.

How to Celebrate

The rite performed is determined by the grieving's religious path and whether they need to express their grief in a Wiccan way. Having said that there are some ritual elements that should always be present. The Western Gate or quarter, ruled by water, is the passageway through which we can let go of our pain. It is also the passageway that the newly freed soul takes to get to the next realm of reality. During the rite, be sure to open the Western Gate to let out the soul who has left and to let the mourners pour their emotions into the powers of the deep sea that stands in the West.

A lovely way to symbolize that someone has gone from this physical world is to have a candle on the altar that represents that soul. As the High Priest and High Priestess release the soul through the Western Gate, they should gently extinguish that flame on the candle. As the flame is extinguished the mourners can release their grief and their best wishes to the soul on its new journey. Normally that particular leftover candle is buried afterward by whoever wishes to take on that task.

Correspondences and Associations

It is very common to associate the color black with death, but white works, too. Black is about the darkness and absence of light that we associate with death. White is about the purity that can come as all colors combine for that soul. Myrrh is a good incense to burn. Sage works well, too.

Timing

When to perform the rites depends on which rites you are performing. The best day of the week for funerary rites is Saturday because it is the day of Saturn. Saturn ruled time, and ultimately death. You may, however, run into funerary laws and funeral home rules on this one. Work that out as best you can. If the funeral service is for a beloved animal, then you can make it happen on Saturday. The same is true if the rite is to be a memorial service. You have a lot of control over that timing. The most appropriate time of day is as close to sunset as possible.

As for the moon, the best time is the waning moon, as close to the darkness of the new moon as possible. Again, if you are performing the actual funeral service, you may not have much control over that issue. Memorial services can be timed closer to the moon's phases.

The Great Rite

This ceremonial rite is not always celebrated and does not ever have to be. It represents the sexual union between the God and Goddess. It should always take place as part of a rite and inside a formal circle. The people performing the rite do this while they are still embodying the deities that they invoked. The rite brings the power of sexual creativity and fertility to the working.

How to Celebrate

The people performing this rite within a circle ritually invoke deity into themselves and come together in a sexual act that is holy. It can be done within a circle privately or publicly, and it can be done in reality, or as we say "in truth" or symbolically. The real act does not need explanation. No matter who is performing the Great Rite in truth, it should be done in full consensual agreement between the people performing the act. Holy act it might be, but if someone is coerced into performing it, it is still sexual abuse.

The symbolic version needs to be described a bit. When performing this version of the Great Rite, the High Priest takes his athame and plunges it into the High Priestess's chalice. This is the rite you will most commonly see performed. It would not be a bad idea to make sure that consent has been discussed before this one is performed as well due to the sexual nature.

Whether you do the rite in truth or symbolically, remember that it is a sacred act that unites the two into one. Traditionally, it was performed by a man and a woman, but in our world today there is much more gender flexibility. Same sex couples can certainly perform the Great Rite and bring the same level of creative power to their working. Solitaires will most likely do the rite symbolically. They should strive to reach for both male and female energies inside themselves while performing the rite.

Correspondences and Associations

The strongest correspondences connected to the Great Rite are the sword or athame and the cauldron or chalice. The sword and athame bring the energy to the act. The cauldron or chalice are the passive receptacles where the energy is converted into reality.

Any colors for the candles will work, but orange is best because it is connected to the sexual energy base of the body. Red and green are good, too. They represent sexual energy and fertility.

Timing

You can do this at any ritual although it is most commonly performed at Beltaine and Samhain. Both sabbats are when the veil between realities is very thin, so the rite carries an extra level of connection between the energies being invoked. Beltaine is a fertility rite, so adding more creativity energy promotes greater fertility. Doing the rite at Samhain can assist the god and goddess in keeping their connection strong at a time of year when they are most separated.

The Great Marriage

This is the rite that celebrates the commitment of the God and Goddess to each other. It is also the act of sex and is often celebrated by a newly handfasted couple on the night of their wedding. This one is also done most often in private because it seals the union of the people involved in the form of the God and Goddess. It should always be done inside a sacred circle because invocation has taken place. And the ritual should also always be performed by two, or more, people who have Perfect Trust between them because it takes personal commitment one step further than the Great Rite. This ritual should never be forced by you or onto you. Consent is always required by everyone who is taking part. Without consent it is abuse, and at that point it is no longer a holy act.

How to Celebrate

If the newly wedded couple, or group, choose to make this level of commitment to each other, then it should be performed inside a formal circle. The participants should invoke deity first. Afterward, be sure to release the deities and open your circle.

Correspondences and Associations

The best associations of this rite are the ones that represent the people involved and their connection to the deities. A large white candle should be at the center. Then surround that candle with candles that represent each person taking part in the rite. The color choice of the candles is made by each individual. Much as in the handfasting, each person should light their own candle. Once all those are lit, as much as possible the participants should come together to light the white candle.

Timing

The timing of this rite, especially if it is performed as part of a handfasting, is dependent on the timing of the marital ceremony. This one takes place later once the festivities are complete. The rite can also be added to anniversary celebrations. The rite can also be added to the Litha sabbat as part of the celebration of commitment.

Moving from Stage to Stage

Something that needs to be added is to address the fear most people have of entering the next stage because it means giving up the one you are in. Not so. Entering a new stage means that you are adding on, not giving up. Because our society worships youth as it does, we are often afraid of the aging process. These rites of passage are set up to assist the growth process through the stages. You do not have to give up the youthful attitudes that you learned earlier. As you age, you can do many of those things better because you are changing perspective.

Another thing to remember is that entering a particular stage of life does not mean that you suddenly have all the wisdom of that stage. The growth through the stage is evolutionary. You enter with only the hint of what the new period means. At the end you understand its fullness and have taken in the power of that age. Recognition that you have taken that power indicates that you are ready to enter the next stage. No one ever completely learns everything. There is always more to learn.

The journey through life's stages are the human equivalent of the journey the God and Goddess take. The God follows the Solar Wheel, and the Goddess has her magick on the Lunar cycles. After all, he is born, knowing he will die, but celebrates life to its fullest. He lives, dies, and is reborn every year. She is ever changing, never dying, like the moon. You see this same progression of the god and goddess in the initiation rites mentioned in the last chapter.

All of these are celebrations and can be used by anyone. Those walking a solitary path can adjust the rites as needed. Tweak and adapt them for what you need. Use them to empower yourself or assist in empowering someone else. And celebrate!

Chapter Eight
FINDING THE DEITY WITHIN YOURSELF

As the priest and priestess hand out cakes and wine at the end of a Wiccan rite, they traditionally say the words, "Thou art Goddess; Thou art God." It is a recognition that each person embodies deity within themselves. If we all contain deity, why do Wiccans use so many different god forms during rituals? We are all trying to reach a state of greater spiritual perfection or enlightenment. Working with and learning the different forms of deity helps us to learn the lessons of the cosmos through example. Understanding how deity manifests externally around you can assist you in accessing and understanding that part of yourself.

Deities and Pantheons

Wiccans generally believe in the duality of the primal force: God and Goddess. Ultimately, there is a single cosmic force behind all of creation, but we divide that force into male and female divinity. From there the division is as complex as you choose it to be. Most commonly, people will honor an earth mother and moon goddess, along with a sun or sky god and the Lord of the Forest, who is often called the Stag King.

The deities with whom you choose to work is often based on what you want to accomplish in a sabbat, esbat, or spellworking. Wicca excels at precision. For example, take the Goddess who is purely female energy. She is like the clear light shined through a prism, and the refracted colors represent Her many aspects. You decide what color or what aspect you want to work with for your work. The difference between Venus and Aphrodite is more than just their different pantheons Roman and Greek. Venus is more voluptuous and sensuous, while Aphrodite is colder and more exacting. Decide what type of love or beauty you want to bring into your life and work with that goddess. If you want to bring about fertility, will you call upon Demeter or Ceres?

Gods are no different. If courage is the key, do you call Thor or Cú Chulainn? Do you want to reconcile with the Underworld and death energies? Is Pluto or Osiris the best god to call upon? It depends on the precise intent of the working as to which aspect you choose. Just remember, that aspect is just that, an aspect of the whole. You are deliberately choosing one piece for precision. Something else to remember, the further back in time you go in choosing a pantheon, the more encompassing the deity will be. The Romans came late, so their deities are very precise energies. The Sumerian deities are much more a gestalt of the overall energy. Venus's energy is extremely defined in how she works in love spells as noted earlier, but if you go back to Astarte or Inanna, then you are looking at much more than just love and beauty.

Invoking Deity

When you choose a deity with whom to work, remember this: the deity is both external and internal. If you are using deity energy to encourage your soul to evolve, then you are attaching the external to that which is already inside yourself. You start this process by invoking a deity. That simply means that you are calling on an energy that is external to yourself to come and work with you, even enter your own consciousness, to assist in your work. As you discover your own internal deity, you will also begin to evoke, or draw forth, that energy from inside yourself to blend with what you have invoked from the external cosmos. When things are going well, those two forces combine inside the witch to make the work happen.

Calling on deity also encourages the evolution of the witch's essence. Each time the energy of a deity joins you from an external point of view that energy attaches to the part of you that has the same power within you. We are so used to viewing deity as something completely external to us that we forget, and sometimes ignore, the godhead within us. Each time you connect with deity you are strengthening that same internal energy within you. Your self-empowerment grows with that growing connection. You are developing the deity that is you and that is one of the primary goals of using deity energy. As your power grows you will find that you are calling less on the external deity and more on the godhead that is you. The gods and goddesses are not threatened by this at all. It is simply the difference between invoking and evoking energy. We call on deity to add to our work what we do not believe we have ourselves. Building that godhead within you means that you call on them less and use your own power more.

Surrender and Sacrifice

Working with deities requires two things, surrender and sacrifice. Surrender comes first. You must surrender to the energy of deity within yourself in order to know what you must change before you can make any kind of sacrifice to bring about that change. Surrendering is hard. You have to stop thinking in terms of the small self and what serves it the best and start thinking in terms of the higher self, the deity within you, and what will force your evolution to even greater heights.

Jesus in the Garden of Gethsemane is the example of surrender with which most of the Western world is familiar. He was praying after having the Last Supper with His apostles. He asked His God to take the cup of sacrifice away from Him, but He ended the prayer with, "Thy will be done". He surrendered to His fate. He knew what was about to happen, and he knew that His higher self needed it to happen. He was arrested at the Garden of Gethsemane and was taken to the road that led to His crucifixion.

We all have the strength within us to surrender to our higher self, but often we stop ourselves even when we know that there are greater things around the corner if we would only give in to the moment, to the greater goal. Why? Fear is the most common reason—fear of the unknown, fear of what we have to give up, or simply fear of change. Timidity is another reason. Surrendering to the unknown brings to the surface a level of personal passion that many folks are too timid to share with the world. If you do get past the timidity, you might become the focus of a person or situation. You hide your passions from the world and yourself so as not to attract attention.

Laziness is also another reason to avoid surrender. It is easier to just stay the same all the time and not reach for something greater. However, it is not satisfying and people who remain stagnant often complain that their lives are empty. Finally, another block to progress is simply the good ol' day-to-day life stuff: bills have to be paid; work has to be done; the people in our lives require our attention. These are all things that become convenient excuses to not surrender to the voice inside your heart that tells you what needs to change and what needs to be sacrificed for the next step to happen.

Once you have surrendered, the sacrifice of whatever is standing in your way becomes easy. Once you have surrendered to a higher part of who you are and the deity within, sacrifice is easy. The surrender is the moment that you touch the deity within you and you gain some knowledge about what must be sacrificed to access more of that energy. That knowledge leads you to the moment when you can make the sacrifice.

Some Important Reminders

When working with deities there are two things to remember. First, be reverent. They are here because you asked them to be, so ask for what you want and thank them. The second is part of that. Never be subservient. You can do something they can't: you can hold all the pieces. We are the microcosm that reflects the whole cosmos. Deities are macrocosms, parts of the whole that is made up of many distinguished pieces. However, they are deities, so use reverence without fear and they will work with you, not against you. Remember, the external deity is a part of your internal god form, so treat that deity and yourself with reference and do not be afraid of what you are becoming.

 ### Exercise
Basic Rite to Make First Contact

You have felt an inner connection to a particular deity. Now it is time to call that deity and make a formal connection.

You will need: candle and incense that corresponds to that deity. You can add oil, cloth, and clothing of the appropriate color.

Gather everything you can that corresponds to that deity. Put those things on your altar. Cast a circle.

Light the candle and incense that is particular to that deity.

Reach inside yourself for the part of you that is that deity. Bring that to the surface of your consciousness.

Invoke the deity that is external to you. Stand at the altar with your arms open and your palms facing upward. Call the deity by name, out loud. Do not use a commanding voice, but a confidant voice.

Once you feel the deity is present, introduce yourself. Ask the deity to join with your internal deity. This is the moment of surrender to the deity inside you. It may take a few minutes, so do not rush the process. Let the two aspects of the deity join inside you.

When you sense that the connection is complete, release the external deity. Be sure to thank the deity. Ground your internal energy. Open your circle.

Thaumaturgy vs. Theurgy

Working with magick is a non-stop question of what kind of witch am I. Are you using magick as a tool to meet an end? Or are you actually stepping more deeply into your own power to achieve the end of self-empowerment? Is what you are practicing practical magick or is it a religion?

Thaumaturgy

Using magick only to perform spells to reach some goal for yourself or others is the practice of thaumaturgy or practical magick.

You may be using Wiccan methods to cast spells, but it is still practical magick or classic witchcraft. Often no deity energy is involved and there is no reliance on a structured religious system. You may hear the titles kitchen witch or hedge mage to describe this type of magickal person. When rituals of any kind are performed, these folks will be there as celebrants. They take part in the energy. They also share their energy with the others.

Choosing to stick strictly to thaumaturgy has its benefits. You are not bound to a deity structure or religion and have no obligations beyond yourself or for whomever you are doing the work. The magick you perform comes from your own will and desire. You can be agnostic or atheist and still use the tools of witchcraft to achieve your goals. You are working for outcomes in the here and now and usually the power and result are immediate. Because you are not tied to a deity or a religion you are far less likely to obsess over the rules that guide your practices, which keeps you from becoming a fundamentalist witch.

There is a downside, of course. You will not have a higher power source other than your own ethical structure. The evolution of the self is not the goal of thaumaturgy so your soul can devolve as easily as it evolves. The power of the magick and the sense of power it conveys to the practitioner can become a trap to keep you doing the same old things over and over again. Whenever you work magick, then no matter what your religious or philosophical beliefs, you are still bound by the Law of Three. The Law of Three is not a downside. Paying the consequences of your actions is not a downside. Not learning from your mistakes and not taking responsibility for your actions are downsides.

Exercise
Thaumaturgist—Protect This Child

A child in your world is under some sort of threat and a protection spell is needed. You decide to make an amulet for the child to wear or carry.

You will need: things you know provide protection; herbs, cloth, and string to make the amulet, a piece of metal, something that represents the love you have for the child.

Inside your sacred space put all the pieces into the cloth then tie it with the string. While doing this fill the amulet with your love. Visualize the child safe and protected by your power.

When you give the amulet to the child, make sure that the child feels your love enveloping him or her. That love makes them feel safe and protected.

Theurgy

Theurgy occurs when the practice of magick is part of an overall religious structure. When you are a theurgist, you recognize deity as part of the magick, both external and internal deity. Theurgists are tied more closely to cosmic forces, or deities. Commonly High Priests and High Priestesses are working theurgists. Their job is to invoke the energy, share the energy, use the energy, then release the energy. Following the idea that Wicca is a mystery religion, the people in the inner circle are usually the ones walking the initiatory path.

Like thaumaturgy, theurgy has an upside and a downside. When evolving spiritual consciousness is your goal, and your magick work is focused on that goal, then evolution is almost a guarantee. Even when you fail at something, you learn the lesson and move forward. You recognize the deity within yourself, which gives a great power source to work your magick. Theurgy gives you access to a myriad of deities, both external and internal and you can call on those powers to work your magick and evolve yourself.

There are also disadvantages. Anyone who practices strict adherence to a set of rules always has the danger of becoming a fundamentalist where the rules become more important than the faith behind the rules. That type of thinking can cut you off from exploring any other magickal avenues. It is also easy to focus on one or just a few deities and ignore all others, which can lead to imbalance. Also, when the magick user's focus becomes imbalanced, then the door becomes open to what is called obsession. Obsession occurs when the imbalanced witch can no longer focus on anything other than one deity. It is the first step that leads to actual possession. The door is now open to that specific energy. The energy can now enter the witch and take over. That is a pretty severe downside in theurgy. Another downside in theurgy is that results can often take longer. Your sense of cosmic backlash makes you weigh any spells you cast very carefully, sometimes too carefully. You might not cast it at all, even when it should be cast.

Exercise
Theurgist—Protect This Child

A child in your world is under some sort of threat and a protection spell is needed. You decide to make an amulet for the child to wear or carry. The only real

difference between this approach and the thaumaturgist approach is that you are going to add deity
energy to the amulet.

You will need: things that correspond to the deity
you have decided to call upon; herbs, cloth, and
string to make the amulet, a piece of metal,
something that represents the love you have for
the child.

Choose a deity who is known for protecting
children.

Cast a circle.

Inside your circle put all the pieces into the cloth.

Before you tie the amulet, invoke the deity, and
ask for their blessing on the amulet. You should also
ask them to bless and protect the child.

Tie the amulet with the string. While doing this
fill the amulet with your love and the love of the deity.
Visualize the child safe and protected by the deity.

Open the circle.

When you give the amulet to the child, make
sure that the child feels your love and the love of the
deity enveloping them. That love makes them feel
safe and protected.

A Combination of Practice

Most witches are both thaumaturgist and theurgist. We tend to
take a middle ground and work with deities, weigh the potential
debt incurred, make self-empowerment a goal, and avoid becoming obsessed or imbalanced during their work. They do not always
work with a group or follow an initiatory path. These are the

witches who show up as celebrants at a rite and gladly share their energy with everyone because they know they will receive that energy back into their lives.

When we invoke a deity, we are working with one particular piece of the cosmos, trying to learn their lesson, their power. Wicca works within the rules of great precision on this one. Ideally, a witch can pull in the precise energy that is needed to learn a particular lesson. The goal is to become more and more balanced, encompassing more of the unity of the cosmos. Each god form is a piece of the cosmos and has its own lesson to teach, but they are each only a part of the greater whole. If you begin to truly incorporate the energies of various god forms, then you start to see a gestalt beginning inside of yourself. Working with the individual god forms gives you more pieces. Later, as the whole begins to come together for you, the pieces become valuable tools for precise work in specific areas. Spellwork for yourself, or others, is easier if you know exactly what energy to call on and work with to accomplish a specific task.

 ## Exercise
The Prism That Is You

You have created a connection between your internal deity in the earlier exercise: Basic Rite to Make First Contact. Now it is time to extend that sliver of the deity to create a gestalt of the varied pieces of that god form. This exercise is aimed at making you the prism through which various aspects of that cosmic energy can be used.

You will need: a clear crystal.

Get a clear crystal. Make sure you have cleansed it thoroughly so it has no energy attached to it. Do some research on the history of the deity with whom you have been connected so that you can understand how that deity splintered over time as the energy was adapted by different cultures.

Cast a circle. Do not invoke any deity. Lay down in the circle. Follow your instincts as to where your head and feet should point. Lay the crystal on your body. Your solar plexus, heart, or third eye are the best places. Let your arms lay beside you, palms facing upward. Relax. Breathe.

Evoke the deity from inside yourself. Visualize that deity's journey through its own history as it began to splinter into pieces. As each piece is defined, call out its name. Once they are all in the circle with you, visualize them joining hands.

The deities while holding hands should begin spinning around the circle. That spinning should get faster and faster until it is impossible to tell one energy from another. At the peak of the spinning, pull all that energy into the crystal. Breathe and rest a minute.

Clasp the crystal in your hands and combine your energy with it. Open the circle. Keep that crystal some place very safe. Use it whenever you need to remind yourself that your power contains all the colors of the prism.

We humans can do something that no deity can do. We can embrace many realities within ourselves. The god forms are capable of seeing only their own particular reality, and no other. They need us as much as we need them. However, that does not mean you can treat a deity with disrespect. They do have dominion over their areas of expertise. When you have achieved some balance inside yourself with these energies, it is a true working relationship.

Chapter Nine
JOURNEYING WITH MEDITATION

Self-empowerment is all about the journey inward. Finding the power within yourself leads to a more fulfilled life. That doesn't mean a life without tough times. It means when the challenges of life come your way, you have the internal power to meet and conquer those challenges. As I have shown, the sabbats, esbats and safe spellcasting can all be used to assist that inward journey. Another tool that can lead to greater awareness of yourself and your internal strength is meditation, which is basically a state of mild hypnosis designed to shut out the world's distraction so we can hear deeper voices. Meditation opens you to the cosmos, and all the energies it contains. Meditation does not belong to Wicca. It is employed to great benefit within many religious and philosophical traditions as well as outside of religion entirely. Witches are no different.

Meditation in Wicca

Wicca has borrowed meditation techniques from other paths and that can be said of most of the world's religions. Meditation as a way to reach the deity within has been around for centuries and is practiced within some of the world's oldest religions and philosophies including Taoism and Hinduism. The use of meditation may predate both of these as well. The tool of meditation is now part of many religions even if it is not always called that, or even consciously recognized as such. Prayer in any religion can be a form of meditation.

You enter this semi-hypnotic state when trying to reach the quiet space within, the clear center or place of inner stability. When in this deep meditative state you can reach the true self. From this place you can make magick happen, whether it is understanding the workings of a particular spell or reaching the awareness of your true will and your connection with the cosmos. It takes work to become proficient at meditation and benefit from its effects. Why do it? Once you are good at meditating, you can learn to better relax in any situation. You can also better contact your higher self and more easily figure out what courses are best in your life and what you can stop worrying about. Finally, you will be able to touch the cosmos at higher levels and use deeper power to energize the spellwork you do.

 Exercise
Creating an Astral Sacred Space

Keep in mind that meditation practice can make you vulnerable, so one of the things you should do early is create your own sacred space, not only in this world, but in the astral world. That space is the doorway through which you will begin each astral journey and through which you will return. It is a safe space that usually only opens to you and to energies that are friendly to you, such as guides.

You will need: music, incense, candles, whatever relaxes you and makes you feel safe.

Close the door to the distractions of the world. Turn off the phone. Get comfortable and relax and let your mind wander. You can use music, incense, candles, whatever relaxes you and makes you feel safe. Do it when time is not critical because it takes as long as it takes.

You have heard the expression, "find your happy space." That is essentially what you are doing. Visualize a place where you have found peace. Do not fill it up with other people. Fill it with things that make you feel safe and happy. A natural setting usually works best, but some urban witches are more comfortable in urban spaces. Just make sure that the only things in your space are yours.

Once you have the space as you want it you need to create a door through which you will enter other realms. It can be an actual door, a waterfall, a path through the woods, a cave opening, whatever signifies to you that you have entered another realm.

When you are ready, leave this sacred space and reenter this reality. You may build this astral space over several meditations. Once it is built that space becomes your doorway into the astral. You can use it as a starting point for all your meditations.

Exercise
Self-Meditation in Practice

Meditation can be practiced in several ways. Self-meditation is a form that enables the user to be dependent on no one or external definitions. The downside of self-meditation is just that you are alone. It becomes easy to become distracted, disappointed, or afraid of what is happening and come running back. There will be no one around to refocus the user or to assist with interpretation later. Although in the end, interpretation is the user's responsibility, not someone else's.

You will need: music, incense, candles, whatever relaxes you and makes you feel safe.

Relax. Light candles and incense if you like. Soft music in the background aids some people in this journey. Do some deep breathing. Enter your sacred astral space. Meditation is not about specific goals, just be open to the journey.

Move toward the doorway that leads to other realms. If a guide of any sort appears, animal or human, let that guide lead you.

Be open to wherever you go and whatever you experience. Just let the images and sensations flow into you. Now is not the time to try to interpret anything.

Once you sense that the journey is over, return to the astral sacred space. Say thank you to any guides who assisted you. Slowly allow yourself to return to this reality.

Once you are fully back to this reality, drink some water, maybe eat a little something. Then write or record your impressions of your meditation. Interpretation will come over time.

Guided Meditation

Guided meditations are in some ways easier and in some ways harder. When you have a guide, whether in person or on a recording, you are less likely to get lost and distracted and give up. The journey will go where the guide takes you and that is the biggest downside of a guided meditation. The guide is directing what happens to a certain degree. However, a well-trained meditation guide will not, and should not, take responsibility for what you, the traveler, experience during the journey. The experiences of the meditation are purely the responsibility of the traveler. The guide is there just to make sure the gates open and the user can get to a place where things can happen.

There can be two types of guided meditation. One type is where the guide takes the traveler through each step and then brings them back. In this type, you will not stray off the mapped territory too much. In the second type, the guide simply opens the gates and invites certain types of experiences to happen and then lets the traveler interact with whatever shows up. No images are projected out to you as in the first type. However, the guide does stay around to make sure things do happen and that you are safe.

Unfortunately, the second type can be difficult for those people who are not used to having visual images appear like this, so they do not really "see" anything even though they may have had a deep experience. For these people, a fully guided meditation, where the images are projected out verbally, is easier. You usually get something out of the experience instantly and do not have to wait for your conscious memory to take effect. If meditation is already tough for you, a fully guided meditation is a good place to start, working up to a semi-guided meditation, and then finally self-meditation.

Prepare for your guided meditation with breathing and relaxing. If you have an actual physical person doing the guiding, then let that person set the stage in terms of music, candles, incense. If you are using a recorded meditation, there may be advice about such things included on the recording. If not, follow your instinct about what works for you. Afterward make notes in your journal about your impressions. If you have done this with a group, talk with each other about those impressions.

Meditation Pitfalls

There are many misconceptions surrounding meditation practice. First, do not expect 3D images complete with script and soundtrack. Holograms are not the common. Most meditations are highly subjective and are composed of images, sensations, ideas, and feelings. Visuals come to some, but most folks get more of a sensation than anything else that may take days to figure out. For some, the full realization comes later in a dream. One way to determine whether a meditation experience has lent you some wisdom is if you suddenly just know something that you did not know before. You cannot tell how you know it or when you learned it, but it is there, and you are sure it is true. Odds are that the new wisdom came during a meditation, found its way to your subconscious, and then rooted into your view of life.

Another misconception is that your meditation should have a focus in a focus or some goal. Just the opposite. The guiding rule is relax and let it happen, no matter what type of meditation you use. Just let the wisdom come to you in whatever form it takes. Interpretation can come later, For the duration of the meditation, let the experience flow over and through you.

A third meditation misconception is that you should immediately be able to flow evenly through the meditation without any distractions from your mind. Not so. The first few minutes of most meditations are about letting the daily stuff go and that is best done by letting it enter, see it, feel it, and then let it flow out of your mind. Do not focus on it and hold it. Don't try to find an answer to it, just let it flow in and then out. This is a way of putting distractions in their proper place so you can see whatever does appear on deeper levels.

Meditation takes practice. Do not beat up yourself or any teacher if it takes a while to get really good at it. Results will most likely not come immediately. Drumming and soft music can assist you in entering the relaxed state that will lead you into your sacred space. Then the images and guides will come. Take your time, set aside time each week to practice. One day, when you least expect it, you will find that your meditation is really taking off and you are getting the desired effect from it.

Exercise
Breathing Technique for
Relaxation before Meditation

Looking at the meditations you have done or plan to do, you will see that most start with deep breathing or similar relaxing exercises. That is there so you can let go of the ordinary and clear the clutter in order to do more extensive work. Do not worry if you fall asleep, many do when they first start meditating. Because many of us get so wound up about day-to-day living, we just fall asleep during the relaxation stage. Here is one technique.

You will need: music, incense, candles, whatever relaxes you and makes you feel safe.

Get comfortable in your real-world sacred space. You can sit or lay down.

Start deep breathing, in through the nostrils, out through the mouth. While you do this visualize breathing in good stuff and breathing out bad stuff.

While still breathing, focus on your body and start relaxing it. Begin with your extremities, feet, and hands. Move up your legs and arms. Relax your lower body, then your chest and neck. Relax your head last.

Astral Journeys

Wiccans often use meditation to quest in the astral for something specific such as spirit animals, patron deities, and magickal names. This type working is commonly called an astral quest or journey. It is best done with a physical guide usually a teacher. That guide can make sure that the seeker does not get lost in the astral and lose track of the goal of the journey. If the quester is a member of a coven, then most commonly the High Priest and High Priestess attend as well. Afterward the guide will spend however long it takes to assist the seeker in interpreting what was seen and experienced. As a note, working with deities can also take the shape of astral quests when looking for answers to questions or seeking guidance. The traveler also may be looking for an astral guide. Solitaires can do this type of journey as well, but there are cautions a solitaire should take. Be sure to do this type of journey in your sacred space. It wouldn't hurt to cast a formal circle. If you have a familiar, let them join you because they are quick to alert you if danger enters the experience. I do not recommend casting a protection spell. That might keep out the very thing you need to experience. Instead just send out a request to the cosmic powers that you have a successful journey.

Astral journeys can take place on the conscious, subconscious, or unconscious. If the meditation is guided, then the journey is a conscious one. In this type of meditation the guide takes the seeker to a particular place on the astral planes and then it goes from there. If an astral guide is the goal, then one is invited to show up. Usually one does and takes charge of the seeker from there. One important note, your astral guide may show up in other types of meditations even if that was not the goal. If your guide shows up at any point, it is best to follow. They have probably been waiting for a long time for you to come to the astral in a conscious way to seek your power.

Astral meditations can also take place on the subconscious and unconscious. The most common way this happens is through what we call the dream state. It can be difficult to determine whether something was a dream or a true astral journey. Lucid dreaming occurs when you are fully conscious of being in a dream state. That is also true of an astral journey. This is when guides, physical or astral, come in handy. If you have had an experience in a dream that confuses you, perform a conscious meditation to the same place with the help of a guide and learn more. Ask questions of your guides but be aware that the answers that you get might be more riddles than anything else. However, answering the riddle is part of the meditation.

Many cosmic energies like to play tricks and outright lie to you as you travel the astral. Deities can appear in the astral. However, some energies will imitate a deity and the trick is to tell which is which. Knowing your correspondences saves a lot of wasted energy on your part. It can even keep you out of dangerous situations such as being obsessed by an energy. Even deities have rules they must follow. Color correspondences are the quickest way to identify deities in the astral. If an energy appears claiming to be Jupiter there to assist you with success, look for the color blue. If no blue is present, it is not Jupiter. The jewelry and metals can also be a giveaway. Venusian energies will have something on them made of copper. As you study your correspondences, learn the sigils for each cosmic energy. If an energy claims to be Mercury, mentally hurl the Mercury sigil at it. If it is not Mercury, it will simply vanish.

Figure 3: Mercury Sigil

Past Life Regression

Another form of meditation is past life regression. Over the course of your life your past lives can surface unbidden in the form of déjà vu. However, you can also explore past lives through an astral journey, during which you can learn more about who you have been so you can correct mistakes of the past. You can also use this type of meditation to better understand the people that come in and out of your current life. You may have had the experience of meeting someone new and just knowing that we have known them before. A past life regression might assist in learning what roles you have played in past lives. That may help define what roles you need to play in this round of existence. Mistakes can be corrected. It is sometimes fun to do the regression with the other person and get their impressions of the old roles. You can compare notes afterward.

There are two cautionary notes about past life regressions. The first is that it is easy to get caught up in memories and forget to live the life you are in now. A good way to avoid that trap, and this is the second cautionary note, is to use an actual guide, a person, in regressions. That person will make sure that when the regression is over, you fully enter this timeline and leave the past where it belongs in the past.

Self-empowerment starts with self. That journey inward is not easy but has the potential to lead you to greater self-awareness, which is a critical part of self-empowerment. Past life regressions, along with astral journeying and other forms of meditation assist the witch on that quest to better themselves at every stage. Never stop relying on meditative techniques, no matter how skilled you are at spellwork. While meditation is not owned by Wiccans, it is certainly a tool that you can and should always use to gain deeper awareness of yourself as you grow and change. This work can only be a positive step to self-empowerment.

Chapter Ten
FAMILIARS

The important role that animals have played in the witchcraft is well-known but mostly misunderstood and misrepresented. Wicca honors and makes use of the power that animals can and do perform. Familiars are awakened animal intelligences and are with you to work magick. They are not your average pet, yet the boundaries do overlap, so be careful how you classify your familiar. A familiar animal should be viewed as a working partner. While you should take care of them and, in many ways, they do operate as pets, the relationship goes past the mundane companionship to something greater.

A familiar attaches to you at some point to aid in its spiritual development. Once an animal attaches to a human, as long as that human is evolving, then the animal's growth is pretty much guaranteed. In return for care and evolution the animal works with you and for you to help your magick. It is the bargain between the familiar and the person. We have a little freedom in terms of picking one out, but it is always better to wait for the familiar to come to you. If you pick one, then you are taking a gamble on that animal. It may or may not be ready to awaken. If it does awaken, then it's ready for work. If it does not awaken, then you have a wonderful, loving pet, but not necessarily a familiar. That is not to disparage the pets out there. They are wonderful animals who give us joy and bring life to our lives. Those animals deserve our respect and honor as much as a familiar, but do not expect the pet to work for you except within the boundaries of what they can do.

If you wait for a familiar to knock on the door, and I have seen that happen, then the awakening has already taken place. That animal has been waiting for a magick user to show up, sometimes you in particular. When I heard that kitten crying underneath my car on a cold, windy night just before Samhain, I had to respond. Sadie the cat came home with me that night and for the next decade she taught me many things. On one notable occasion after I moved, she expressed her displeasure with her witch by taking a pee in my cauldron. I listened, there just wasn't much I could do to change the situation. Once the familiar has found you, a working relationship can start.

Getting to Know Each Other

After a beautiful little animal has picked you out and you have made a bargain with it to mutually care and evolve together, what do you do next? First, choose its name. Try to let the animal tell you its name. It is all too easy to just pick a name and make it stick and never really know the animal's real name. Sometimes the animal speaks so clearly that the name you hear is the one that is right. Sadie spoke loudly on that car ride home that I knew her name immediately. How do you know? If it is the right name, the animal will answer to it right away.

I saw a young Wiccan get the correct familiar, who had made it clear he was meant to be with this young man. Then the young witch tried very hard to give the kitten a name that just was not what the familiar was about at all. Another witch walked in and with no prior attachment called the little guy by his proper name, and everyone knew it was right, even the familiar's own witch knew it was right. Give it some time, and it may take a few weeks, but let the animal tell you. Do not expect it to jump in your lap and say a word. It may come as an image, an action that the animal constantly performs, a dream, or many other ways. Once you have heard the right name, there will be no question in your mind. Not only that, but you have just learned the first thing that the familiar has to teach you: how to listen to it. Familiars do not speak human; you have to learn to listen to the way the animal speaks.

As I discussed, the witch's part of the bargain is to care for the animal, but what do familiars do for us? Lots. They can bring and carry messages because they work in the astral extremely well. They do not have blocks to moving through different realities. They read energy patterns around us, better than we do. They point out problems and mistakes. They are often more aware of magickal flow around us than we are. Why? Animals do not interpret what they experience. They do not have all that powerful upper brain function getting in the way of their instinctive responses. They just react to what they see and feel. They respond to things from their perspective without the energy blocks that we humans have learned to use, often to the detriment of our own instinctive responses.

Think of the last time an animal of yours reacted to someone new in your life. Was it a positive or negative response? Did you listen? Or did you let your polite training take over, even when your own instincts told you to flee? Sadie taught me so much about this issue. She was very clear about people. She did not like many people. She often did not like me. The two people that she had an unexpected and extreme fondness for turned out to be two of the most important people in my magickal world. She saw something that I might have missed if I did not pay attention to her. Familiars interact with the world and the energies of the world from the perspective of animals. They listen first to their instinctive responses and respond appropriately. That is what they are telling you to do in many situations.

Once you start working with a familiar, you both have to grow. It usually takes a familiar three to four years to really start using their power in a way no one can miss. They will often show hints of it early on, so watch what they do and see how they respond to people and things. Eventually, they will show you where their talents lay, but always remember, it will be from their perspective, not yours.

Familiars are also reflections of who you are and what your talents are. They will assist you as you grow into those talents. If you have a dog who really has a talent for moving energy, you probably do as well. Watch how the dog does it and copy. They do it better than us because they do not block their moods and emotions and instincts. If your normally friendly parakeet suddenly does not like someone, pay attention. Do not automatically cut that person out of your life, because they may have something that you need to learn, but be aware of their energy pattern, because that little bird saw something.

 Exercise
Opening Up to a Familiar

Following is an exercise to help you open your magickal life up to working with a familiar.

You will need: yourself and your familiar.

Love the animal. Sounds simple, but that is the first step. Do not start the relationship based on your expectations. Just let the bond of love grow between you. Along with that, let trust form between you.

During quiet moments of interaction with your familiar, relax and let images flow into your mind. This is a form of meditation. In fact, if possible, let your familiar join you during your meditations. Cats and reptiles often really enjoy meditations. If your familiar is more active, like a dog, then those active times serve the same purpose. Let the images, and with dogs interacting with you they are often images of joy, fill your mind.

Examine the images that your familiar sent to you. That is how they most commonly will speak with you. If you got a clear direction about something, follow through on that advice. As much as possible, let the familiar know that you followed through and how it turned out.

Talk with your familiar, long conversations about everything. The images and their actions will be their part of the conversation.

Other Types of Familiars

Familiars come in forms beyond cats, dogs, and other common animals. Here are a few other types of familiars that you may want to work with or encounter.

Greater Familiars

Greater Familiars are familiars that take the relationship between the animal and human to a higher level. This familiar usually starts out its journey with you as any other familiar. It appears in your life, first as a beloved pet. Then it becomes obvious that it is a familiar. It is over time that you recognize some differences from other familiars you have or have had. A Greater Familiar's lessons are hard. They are stern taskmasters. If you fail to learn the lesson or hear the advice of a familiar, then they display disappointment but also patience. Greater Familiars have no patience. You fail, you are likely to get clawed or bitten.

Greater Familiars are usually attached to things that we have carried around for years and have to work really hard to get rid of to get to deeper levels of our power. Sometimes Greater Familiars have their own agenda that is past what a regular familiar is doing, like they are former teachers of ours from other lives, or they have a debt to work off from some transgression in their former life. Whatever their issue is, you will know by the time the animal is about five if there is something else going on besides the regular business of a familiar. Sadie was halfway through her life when she let me know that she was a former teacher who was basically taking a break. That is often what a Greater Familiar is doing, taking a break. They still work, but their needs are met without much effort on their own part. It is a rest between hard-working lifetimes.

Familiars in Spirit Form

Sometimes the loving relationship between a witch and a familiar extends beyond one lifetime. A familiar that has passed on may show up for you in spirit form. This is most likely to happen when you are dealing with issues that particular familiar worked on with you during its life.

If you are struggling with an old issue yet once again and you feel the presence of a beloved familiar, trust your own power. That creature is there to assist and guide you once again. Give yourself over to the love and respect that you still have for that creature. Their communication may be even clearer than it was when they were in physical form.

Human Familiars

On a more negative note, human familiars do occur. This is one you will not see many magick users talking about because they just do not want to acknowledge that this can and does happen, but it does. The whole situation is the same as an animal familiar, except we are talking about a person who has chosen to attach to a more powerful witch to insure his/her evolution. It means a lot less work for the familiar. As long as the witch is evolving, so is the familiar. These situations can last a long time, or a short time. The most positive thing I have ever witnessed in this situation was when a young witch learned to the point where he was able to break the relationship himself. It was a positive outcome.

These situations occur when free will is involved. If someone freely chooses to become someone else's familiar, then who are we to judge? Usually if someone chooses, by their own free will, to become a familiar, then the two people are making a sort of contract. Now, if the more powerful person is forcing the relationship to go that way, well, they will pay the price for removing someone else's free will choice. When the time comes for the human familiar to break free, if the other person truly cares about the familiar, then they will let them go with no hesitation. Both parties benefit and grow.

Exercise
Creating a Bond Beyond Death

The time has come to let a familiar move to their next stage. It is not a happy time, but it happens. If you have the advantage of seeing this coming, here is something you can do to keep their wisdom in your life.

You will need: yourself and your familiar.

Make sure the familiar wants to create this level of bond. Spend some time with them and ask. By now you should have a good flow of communication between you. If the answer is yes, go to Step Two.

If at all possible, be with the familiar at the moment of death. Like humans, the spirit hangs around for a bit. Hold that familiar close to your heart and feel its spirit as it breaks free of the physical world.

Once you are sure the spirit is free of the flesh, call out to it and pull it into your own spirit.

Cautionary note: Do not let your own desire to keep the familiar with you override the familiar's desire. If they do not wish to do this, then let them go free.

Saying Goodbye to a Familiar

It happens. Animals do not have the life spans that humans do. And it hurts. We have all lost a beloved pet and it is like losing a family member. When you lose a working magickal partner, it is painful, but it is also part of the bargain. If the animal's evolutionary goals have been met, and their witch has gotten where he/she was headed, it is time for the little animal to move on. Now they can pursue their growth to the next step. If a familiar has told you it is time for them to go, then let them.

Do not forgo health care, however, when one of your animals is sick, for Goddess's sake. Sometimes they are not really ready to go and are fixable. At the same time, if one is showing signs of passing, sit and talk with them and listen. By now you and that animal have established a communication pattern. Ask them if they are ready. They will answer. If the answer is yes, then let them choose the method. Some will slip quietly away in their sleep. Some will need a vet's assistance, or yours. It is their choice and their final lesson to you. Feel free to mourn them properly. They, too, were members of the family and magick users in their own right. Honor them as such. Sadie was with me only ten years. When she passed, she was mourned by quite a few witches.

After they pass, familiars will often show up for a while to reassure you that they are okay, and you should be okay, too. Those spirits floating through always make me both happy and sad. Sometimes they remain familiars, only in spirit form, at least for a while. When my familiar Katchina, who partnered with me for twenty years, passed, she was really gone, not so much as fleeting spirit in my world. I figured she had done her work and was taking a well-deserved break. After a year had passed, I was moping around because I could not celebrate a rite in the way I wanted to do. I was seriously moping. Suddenly there was Katchina! She was still the lovely little gray cat she had always been. She was very clear in her message. "Get up off your butt and light a candle. If after all these years you cannot get a circle up and running with one candle, then we both have more work to do." Familiars can and do show up in spirit form, even if they are not around in physical form. You just have to pay attention to the dreams or whispers that come along to aid in your growth.

When the mourning period is over, wait to see who turns up next to work with you. Because someone will. There are always more lessons to be learned and more familiars with whom to work. Be open to who knocks on the hotel room door, or who calls out in the parking lot in a very loud voice, or who is sitting in a cage at a flea market. Hear them when they call to you and each of you will grow and rejoice in the magick.

Exercise
Mourning for a Familiar

Mourning for a familiar is not very different from mourning for a human. You can do a formal memorial service or funerary rite or keep it simple. The exercise below is a private mourning rite.

You will need: a picture of the familiar, some of the things that the familiar loved, toys, bedding, food, incense, maybe myrrh, a candle, black if you wish, but choose a color that makes you feel close to your familiar.

Get it all together in your sacred space. Light the incense and the candle.

Relax. Whisper your familiar's name. Take yourself down the trail of memories of the time the two of you shared. Cry.

When you are done, blow out the candle. You can bury it with the familiar if you wish. You can also keep it and burn it whenever you need to feel the love you had for that familiar.

Do not let anyone tell you it is silly to mourn for an animal. If they have never felt that kind of loving bond with an animal that is their problem. Do not let it become your problem.

Familiars Make Stronger Witches

Animals in general bring many gifts to the humans who create bonds of love and trust with those animals. Animals ease loneliness, make us smile, teach children responsibility, promote better health, and fill our reality with something other than our daily cares. Personally there have been times in my life that the only thing that got me out of bed was the need to care for those innocent creatures.

When that relationship goes to the level of a witch and a familiar then the possibility of developing a stronger witch emerges. You hate getting up in the morning. Then you uncover your avian familiar and it starts to sing that beautiful morning song. Suddenly mornings are not quite so bad. You are struggling to find any joy in your life. Your canine familiar bounces through your home or yard with such joy that you feel happier. You are so sad because someone in your life has rejected your growing self-definition. Your feline familiar snuggles up next to you and purrs. It is comfortable with its own definition. That is when you know you can maintain the truth of your identity. It has been a while since your magick showed any signs of working. Your reptile familiar looks deep into your eyes. You are reminded of the depth of your power and find the patience to let the magick work. You are struggling with feelings of just not fitting in with any group. You watch your amphibian familiar move easily through different environments in its terrarium. That is when you know you have the ability to fir in wherever you find yourself.

It often takes tremendous inner strength to stay true to our self-definition and our magickal journey. Familiars are animals who never vary from the truth of their path. They remind us to always stay true to ourselves. They can show you how to access your inner strength and power. The bonds of love and trust between the witch and the familiar are the map of following the directions the familiar gives you. Your strength will expand as you follow those directions.

People who practice magick in most forms are likely to draw animals to them. The relationships that the witch and the animal form are as important as the human relationships that get formed in life. Always remember that these are working relationships and the animals need respect as much as they need love and care. Honor the animals who turn up in your life. They can do much to enhance your magick.

Chapter Eleven
TAKING YOUR POWER

You picked up your wand and started riding your broom some time ago, but you have been hesitant to let your identity as a witch and Wiccan become public. Those close to you know. You do have concerns, however, about how this will be received by the greater community. Will it affect your job? Will friends who are not part of your inner circle accept you? Will you be shunned at group events that are not based on religious choices? These are all valid concerns even in our world today.

Being true to your identity is a big step in taking your power. Getting past fear and shyness about that identity is a form of empowering yourself. Another part of taking that power is how you choose to become more public about who you are. You do not need to take a full page ad out in the local newspaper. You do not need to march into school or your workplace covered in witchy accoutrements waiting for someone to challenge you. You do need to answer truthfully if asked about that simple pentagram necklace you are wearing. You do need to explain, if asked, why when the food is blessed you begin your prayer with Lord and Lady. Seizing your power as a witch means that you stay true to your definition whenever the external world questions that choice.

If you encounter negative responses to your religious choice, do not give them your power by letting that response upset you. Stay true to your own self-definition. That is empowering.

Coming Out of the Broom Closet

Coming out of the broom closet is a big decision and has many layers. It is also an ongoing decision. You will face many situations where you have to debate inside yourself how much to reveal. How you make those decisions is part of the journey to greater personal power. Finding yourself in a gathering where the response would likely be negative, it is great power to remain silent. Never deny the truth of who you are, but being a powerful witch means you answer questions diplomatically. If not asked, be powerful by saying nothing.

Whether you are working with a coven or circle or working as a solitaire you have made a step in your journey to self-empowerment as a witch. You may be a thaumaturgist, who uses the tools of witchcraft to build your internal power and faith in yourself. You may have decided to walk an initiatory path as a theurgist and your magicks are focused on self-evolution. No matter which path you take, at some point it will become obvious to the people in your world, if it hasn't already, that you are doing some things differently than you have in the past.

Friends and Family

If you have yet to be public with your identity, whether you are new to witchcraft or have been at it a long time, you must decide how to introduce this new you to your family and friends. Loading yourself down with pagan jewelry, dressing in black from head to toe, and attending the next family reunion or family religious gathering may not be the best way to let the world know that you are now a witch. Unless you just enjoy those kinds of conflicts. For most of us the easiest way is one step at a time, waiting for what we and those closest to us are ready to deal with. Friends usually come first because they see you in many social situations. Some friends really do not care, as long as you remain true to the person they have come to love over time. Some friends will run away, but the question has to be, what kind of friend was that anyway?

Family may be harder to approach, because they may have more of a personal stake in your salvation. It is usually best to just let them see over time who you are and who you are becoming. When they ask why you do not attend religious services with the family anymore, take it from there. Sometimes their fear will make them say and do things that are not pleasant, but again, let them see who you are, a good and decent person. Usually they will take you back into the family's embrace. Some may never be happy with your religious choice, but most will reconcile over time that you are still a decent person. If they say they are praying for you, say thanks. After all, their god is one of the gods and assistance is always welcome.

When friends and family are hostile, it can hurt and if they abandon you, it will be difficult to lose them. But keep being the best you can be and continue your growth. They have their own true will to follow and, if they aim to harm you, they will pay the cost for any negativity they aim at you. The Law of Three does not just apply to witches. Everyone has to answer for the actions they take. The worst two things you can do are to pretend to be something you are not and to throw what you are in their face in a negative way. The inner strength you have gained will lend you the power to walk away from negative responses with dignity and grace.

Coming out of the broom closet was easy for me. I had always been the weirdo at home and at school. My being a witch didn't really surprise anyone. My sister's reaction came wrapped in two different gifts. She, her sons, and I had a tradition of going camping together in the summer and it was during one of these trips that the first gift came. She bought me a small cauldron. When she gave it to me, she said, "It's a little bitty cauldron so you can cast little bitty spells." It was sort of a joke, but it indicated that she knew I was serious.

Years passed and my sister and I stayed close. She watched my growth and joy as I walked the witchy pathway. The year before she died, she gave me one last gift—a T-shirt that said, "I haven't been the same since that house fell on my sister." Watching the movie *The Wizard of Oz* was a very special childhood memory for us. She knew her time was short and that the t-shirt would remind me to always stay true to my faith. I wore it until it was in tatters. What I have said to anyone who wanted to challenge my religious choice is that I will not deny who I am to make them comfortable. I have never spit my choice in anyone's face, but if my choice makes them uncomfortable, then that is their problem, not mine.

Coming Out in Public Forums

Coming out in the public forum is another issue altogether. The legal ramifications are discussed later in this chapter. However, I will discuss public presentation here. Once you have made the decision to be completely out of the broom closet you will choose the public venue with which to start. Each public area of your world offers different challenges and rewards. Coming out in a school setting might well offer some backup. Odds are your friends already know. Some of them may even be witches themselves. Let your social group know that you are about to go public. Wear that pentacle to school. Or cast a simple spell to aid you in passing an exam. Answer questions honestly, but simply. It is easier to go public in college because there is such a large and diverse population. You might even make new friends.

The easiest way to come out at work is over holidays. Wiccan holidays are slightly different to the holidays celebrated by the larger society. Go to whoever schedules the work force. Tell them that you are willing to work Christmas Day if you can have Yule as your day off. The conversation that follows will allow you to go public at your job. You can place some small symbol of your religion on your desk, as long as you follow the same guidelines everyone must follow.

The more general public world of restaurants, shopping, walking in the park, etc. offer other areas to be a public witch. Your choice of jewelry and fashion are a visual signal to others. Some will notice, some will not. If you are asked about the meaning of something like a pentacle, answer honestly and with grace. There is no need for a long lecture unless they want one.

Passing is a term you do not hear as much in the craft as you use to, but it still applies. Passing simply means that you look and act like everyone else. Learn how to keep a low profile when you do not want to draw attention to yourself. When you want to draw attention, then learn how to deal with it from a place of peace and positive energy. Show the world that we are decent folks with a different pathway, then you will be spreading positive energy.

Responding to Backlash

Let's say you are walking down the street, not doing anything particular, and then someone shouts "Witch!" at you in a hostile way. What do you do? You are in a restaurant and someone at another table decides to take issue with you because of your jewelry or something they overheard in your conversation. Do you respond?

The best thing to do in such situations is ignore them. If they persist in persecuting you, be the better person and walk away. Getting into arguments and trying to convince others that you are right, makes you just as negative and closed-minded as they are, doesn't it? If they insist on taking it to that level, just shut them out. This is when protective spells come in very handy. Do not aim negative energy at them, just make yourself an undesirable target. My own favorite is to create something more interesting for them elsewhere, like an entire table falling over in another part of the restaurant, without anyone getting hurt of course. Or learn some basic shrouding techniques so you just are not that noticeable.

Exercise
The Waiter Dropped a Tray

Imagine that you and your friends are enjoying coffee and having a lively discussion about magickal practices. Or maybe you are alone having coffee and reading a book about witchcraft. Either you or the group sense some negative attention coming your way. It is time to create a distraction that avoids a hostile interaction with someone.

You will need: yourselves. Note that the following is set up for a group, but you can do it all by yourself, too.

Once you are all in agreement of where to aim some energy, start joining your energy together. You can do this by joining hands.

As one of the wait staff comes through the tables with a tray filled with water, aim your collective energy at the tray. Water works best because it cannot spill and burn anyone. Do not aim at the waiter because you do not want that person to fall down.

As the tray comes in proximity to the table that is sending negative vibes toward you, let the energy flow in a stream toward the tray. The tray becomes imbalanced, and the water hits the floor.

No one gets hit or hurt, but the clatter and ensuing cleanup draw attention away from you or your group. Now you can enjoy the rest of your conversation or book.

Exercise
Not the Pumpkin You're Looking For

Basic shrouding is not so much about being invisible as it is about just not standing out. You want to do some shopping and you are wearing jewelry that marks you as a witch. You can remove the jewelry and in some situations that might be preferable. However, if fear and maybe shame are making the decision to hide your truth, take your power and shroud instead.

You will need: yourself.

Before you enter whatever shopping arena, find a quiet spot and focus on whatever is making you stand out as a witch.

Use your powers of visualization to make that object or objects appear like something a non-witch would wear.

As you encounter people meet them eye to eye, and smile. If they start conversations with you about everyday affairs, be polite but move on as quickly as you can.

If someone really sees past your shrouding and starts a positive conversation with you, you might have met someone you want to get to know.

Practice shrouding when there is a gibbous moon because shrouding is a form of shapeshifting.

Moving On

As you grow and evolve and come closer to your true will, you may find that someone who was okay with you as a witch when it was just some quirky thing you were doing by yourself, but it is not okay with you when you reach into the world and grow past your fears and self-deceptions. This is one of the hardest things to face as a witch. Sadly, many of the relationships we form over time are based on the insecurities and negative self-images we and the others have. When we begin to break free of those things, we see that the other person cannot follow, or the other person decides the relationship is not giving them what they are used to having.

Every step we take toward greater self-empowerment is always a risk and it always entails that one's self-image be redefined. In the end that is the toughest part of personal growth and pursuing that true will. You become a better, more powerful person, but those old fears and self-deceptions sure were comfortable. It takes great courage to give up a comfortable self-definition, no matter how negative it is, and risk whatever the new definition will be. A true friend or loved one is the one who supports your growth no matter what the risk to the relationship. Coming out of the Broom Closet forces you to take the risk in order to pursue your true will and self-empowerment.

Solitaire, Circle, or Coven

We all started walking the witch way in some form. As a solitaire you may have started through books or online readings. You might have taken classes at a local venue. In today's world you may have even been raised as a Wiccan. You have worked alone. You have worked with groups. Each change in your life often led to a change in how you chose or had to work, whether with others or as a solitaire.

As surprising as it may be, one of the biggest questions you will consistently ask yourself over and over again is whether you want to practice witchcraft by yourself or with a group of people. There are a lot of variables involved in making this decision, and you may choose different things at different times. Celebrating the sabbats and esbats may make you want a group, while certain types of spells and internal work may take you down the Solitaire's path. Sometimes sheer convenience plays a role. Is there even a group available for you? In time you may be called on to be the one who starts the group. There are a lot of considerations in making this choice and it is one you will make over and over.

There are advantages and disadvantages to all three of the choices. Your decision at any given moment may revolve around those advantages and disadvantages. Here are some basic definitions and details about all three, but in the end the choice will always be yours to make.

Solitaire

To a certain degree we are all solitaires because there is no central doctrine in Wicca except for the Wiccan Rede. We all make our own ethical rules for how we will exercise our power in this reality. Certainly when you cast many spells and often in celebrating esbats you will do that work as a solitaire even when you are involved with a circle or coven. A true solitaire, however, does not work with a group except on rare occasions. Often not even then do they give completely of their energy because they have no pattern to follow in doing so. There are advantages and disadvantages to being totally on your own.

Advantages

Probably the greatest advantage of working totally as a solitaire is that your energy is not linked with anyone else's. You are free to make your own decisions and are not responsible for the decisions others make.

You also have no responsibility to anyone else when you do make a decision. There will not be anyone else around to say no when you are sure you are following your true will. In the end your decisions are completely your own without anybody else voicing an opinion.

Disadvantages

A solitaire has no backup if something goes wrong, or if they are making a poor decision. There is no moral compass available to gauge if you are following true will or the desires of the smaller self.

When you are practicing alone, it becomes very easy to avoid the very lessons you most need and hide behind your fear and not do the hard things, even when that would be the most beneficial thing to your growth and evolution. When the going gets tough, you will have no other magick user available to lend their energy to you for the hard spots. If you do try this way out, remember these pitfalls.

If you have always worked with a group, then some time as a solitaire might assist you in reaching deeper into your personal power. Give the solitary practice a try for a year and day. See what your power does when relying totally on yourself.

Circle

A circle is a group of Wiccans and other magick users who agree to come together to do certain types of spellwork and celebrate the sabbats and the esbats. They are usually led by High Priests and/or High Priestesses. This is an excellent format for teaching because these witches come together to celebrate holidays and degree advancements. Circles can also be used as a screening tool for people who are looking for their path but have not yet made a decision. The numbers are usually, and work best, when kept at twenty or below. Being part of a formal circle usually does not involve taking vows.

Advantages

The big one here is that you have a built-in support group when the growth path gets hard. You have that constant moral compass to assist in tough decisions. The circle will assist in learning how not to take yourself too seriously and not to block up on life's decisions so you can make better decisions that express your personal power in a positive way. In working with a circle you will have less of a tendency to get stuck in routine work and get stuck with bad habits in the rites, or in life.

Circles are quite possibly the best format for students and teachers to work together in. In circle work there is usually a constant flow of people in and out, so you will learn how to generously share your energy and also have a teacher to assist in that lesson. If you are solitary, circles are a great introduction to group work; to test the waters so to speak. If you have worked within a group before, attending circle gatherings is way to try out different traditions that might suit you better or help expand your magickal education.

Disadvantages

You will have energy bonds to other people and their decisions, particularly if you sit there and let someone else make a really bad decision without attempting to advise them. You do have a responsibility to share your energy with the rest of the circle. There will be people in the circle that you do not like on a personal level, but you are around them during circle gatherings. The guiding rule here is that you do not have to be socially friends with all these people, but respect that everyone is there because they are following a path of personal growth and trying to be positive people. If you came to working with a circle after being solitary, part of your growth path may well be how to handle just such situations. Another thing that solitaires may need to learn is that if you throw your problems out to the circle, expect honest responses from the members. This is something you have not dealt with before.

Finally, and maybe silly sometimes, but often the most annoying thing about working with a group is that you are always trying to find times that are as convenient as possible for as many people as possible. It is always a drop five and punt situation. The rule of thumb is that whoever is running the particular event sets the time that works best for them. Then the needs of their teacher and High Priest and High Priestess get met. Everyone else deals with it as best as possible.

Coven

A coven is a tight knit group with a history and an agreement on the way they will practice and the way the rites are celebrated. They have willingly entered into a cosmic bond with the other coven members and have taken vows of commitment to the coven and its members. The group is usually thirteen to fifteen people, although smaller is often seen. The group is led by a High Priest and/or a High Priestess. When someone else is ready to enter into that title, then a hiving occurs, and the new High Priest or High Priestess begins another coven elsewhere with any members that are ready to move on. Hopefully the hiving will take place peacefully and with the blessing of the original coven. In this type of group the elders and teachers tend to take back roles and have usually passed the Wand of leadership on to the current High Priest and/or High Priestess.

Advantages

You always have the coven to rely on when you are in distress and need support. They are bound by vows to support you and will suffer consequences if they do not. There is a standard set of rules that govern you all. The rules of the coven can be changed by group vote, but they are the standard for everyone in the coven.

The coven will always be working on a magickal pathway, even if it gets really hard. The only way to escape for the individual is to formally leave the coven, which does involve recanting the coven vow. A coven can also be formally disbanded if all the members agree. If you have been working either solitary or even with a circle, this is a great way to deepen your magickal bonds and create a powerful trust in community with other witches toward a shared goal. Strength in numbers is not just a saying.

Disadvantages

You are vowed to be available with your energy and will suffer retribution if you break that vow. You can formally remove yourself from the coven and you have to do that if you are not willing to honor your vow. It is not a positive thing to try to pick and choose when you are available and when you are not. Part of that disadvantage is that if you betray your coven or your vows to it, then you can be removed from the coven. Each coven will have its own way of doing that, but it most likely will not be pleasant and can lead to some very hurt feelings on everyone's part.

You are cosmically bound to the coven members and if they mess up and you could have prevented that, then you will take part of the responsibility for that negative action. That is not escaped by saying, "I wasn't around when that happened." Coven members should know each other well and should be willing to assist each other's growth so that decisions made by each member as individuals are the best that person can reach at that particular stage of growth.

Covens can stagnate because there is not the constant flow of new people and ideas into it. Coven members should always be looking for ways to continue to grow and not sit on their laurels so that the coven can grow and evolve over time. That is where voting means a lot. New ideas are introduced and voted on. Bad hivings start when tyrannical leadership takes over and will not allow anything new into the door, or even will not hear out the ideas of the other coven members.

To Group or Not to Group

In the end it is always your choice and may vary over time based on where you are in your growth path. You can make a new decision at any point in time, but always be sure of what best serves your growth path and make sure that others in circles and covens are aware of what your decision is. Group work has its joys, especially during the sabbats and degree rites, but you will not always be willing or able to share that much of your life. On the other hand, being a solitaire, while not quite as time consuming, can lead to boredom and the desire to share with others the joy of Wicca and its energy. The big one is do not try to be all of the above all of the time. Be completely there for the group if that is what you choose. If you want to work alone for a while, then be a solitaire. Do not be afraid if you need to do one for a while and then do the other. The cosmos will send you what you need when you need it, just be willing to listen and follow through.

Are You a Wiccan Witch?

Wiccan witches do not have a central doctrine to which we all adhere. The only thing you will find that we all tend to agree with is the Wiccan Rede, "And it harm none, do what thou wilt." The Rede is connected to the idea that all of our actions, good and bad, return to us threefold, the Law of Three. In addition to the Rede, many witches also agree to the thirteen "Principles of Wiccan Belief." The Council of American Witches, which was active from 1973 to 1975, was an alliance of Wiccans from a variety of traditions. This council drew up the thirteen principles in 1974. They read as follows:

Principles of Wiccan Belief

1. We practice rites to attune ourselves with the natural rhythm of life forces marked by the phases of the moon and the seasonal quarters and cross-quarters.

2. We recognize that our intelligence gives us a unique responsibility toward our environment. We seek to live in harmony with nature, in ecological balance offering fulfillment to life and consciousness within an evolutionary concept.

3. We acknowledge a depth of power far greater than is apparent to the average person. Because it is far greater than ordinary, it is sometimes called "supernatural," but we see it as lying within that which is naturally potential to all.

4. We conceive of the Creative Power in the Universe as manifesting through polarity—as masculine and feminine—and that this same creative Power lives in all people, and functions through the interaction of the masculine and feminine. We value neither above the other, knowing each to be supportive of the other. We value sexuality as pleasure, as the symbol and embodiment of Life, and as one of the sources of energies used in magickal practice and religious worship.

5. We recognize both outer worlds and inner, or psychological worlds—sometimes known as the Spiritual World, the Collective Unconscious, the Inner Planes, etc.—and we see in the interaction of these two dimen-

sions the basis for paranormal phenomena and magickal exercises. We neglect neither dimension for the other, seeing both as necessary for our fulfillment.

6. We do not recognize any authoritarian hierarchy, but do honor those who teach, respect those who share their greater knowledge and wisdom, and acknowledge those who have courageously given of themselves in leadership.

7. We see religion, magick, and wisdom-in-living as being united in the way one views the world and lives within it—a world view and philosophy of life, which we identify as witchcraft or the Wiccan Way.

8. Calling oneself "witch" does not make a witch—but neither does heredity itself, or the collecting of titles, degrees, and initiations. A witch seeks to control the forces within themself that make life possible in order to live wisely and well, without harm to others, and in harmony with nature.

9. We acknowledge that it is the affirmation and fulfillment of life, in a continuation of evolution and development of consciousness, that gives meaning to the Universe we know, and to our personal role within it.

10. Our only animosity toward Christianity, or toward any other religion or philosophy-of-life, is to the extent that its institutions have claimed to be "the one true right and only way" and have sought to deny freedom to others and to suppress other ways of religious practices and belief.

11. As American witches, we are not threatened by debates on the history of the Craft, the origins of various terms, the legitimacy of various aspects of different traditions. We are concerned with our present, and our future.

12. We do not accept the concept of "absolute evil," nor do we worship any entity known as "Satan" or "the Devil" as defined by Christian tradition. We do not seek power through the suffering of others, nor do we accept the concept that personal benefits can only be derived by denial to another.

13. We work within nature for that which is contributory to our health and well-being.

In reading the Thirteen Principles it is easy to see that those you know who practice the Wiccan religion do follow these principles even if they cannot quote them all or know they exist. However, they are also very general statements and all Wiccans will have more precise ways of worshipping, often depending on which specific pathway that person follows.

Wicca and Religious Freedom

Taking your power as a public witch or Wiccan comes with responsibilities. Your first responsibility is to yourself and your truth. Second, like it or not, now that you are public, you are a representative for all of us. Wear your truth with dignity in every venue.

Do not break the basic rules that apply to everyone at your workplace or your school. If no one can wear religious jewelry, then neither can you. If no one can burn incense at their desk, then neither can you. However, when is the line crossed between simple rules that everyone must follow and true discrimination against you because you are following a religious tradition that others find objectionable and frightening?

There are resources to find answers to that question and to get assistance when true discrimination occurs. The first step is for you to understand what your rights are under the law in your country. The United States has very well-defined legal structures at the federal level. If you are a U.S. citizen, then you must also find out what the laws are at the state and local levels. When you are doing research at the state and local level, then the rule is simple. Those levels of government cannot pass any laws that contradict the law at the federal level. Beyond that, here are some guiding principles for the United States.

The First Amendment

The First Amendment of the Constitution of the United States, the federal government's position on religious freedom, states clearly, "Congress shall make no law respecting an establishment of religion or prohibiting the free exercise thereof; or abridging the freedom of speech, or of the press; or the right of the peoples peaceably to assemble, and to petition the government for a redress of grievances."[5]

What the amendment means is that we all have the right to worship as we feel led and not be forced to worship in someone else's way. That does not mean the right to commit any illegal acts toward others, or to break the law and call it religion. The courts have been very clear on this one. An illegal action is just that, illegal. You cannot kill another person and claim that you were performing a religious act of sacrifice. Murder is still murder.

---

5 First Amendment U.S. Const.

Wicca Recognized

In 1986 a Federal Court found that Wicca was a religion under the definition of religion and had to be afforded the same rights and privileges of any other religion in this country. That decision meant that no one could ever take a legal stand against Wicca as a non-religion unless they were prepared to go all the way to the Supreme Court and win. Being classified by the Federal Court as a religion gave Wiccans the ability to call on the first and fourteenth amendments from that point onward.

The definition of Wicca as a religion that the courts have relied on came from the US Army's *Religious Requirements and Practices of Certain Selected Groups: A Handbook for Chaplains*. The *Handbook* first recognized Wicca as a religion in 1978. The US military has recognized Wicca as a religion and allowed its practice in the various branches ever since. The *Handbook* has a wonderful definition for laypeople.

Being classified as a religion by the Courts gave us access to the fourteenth amendment as well as the first. Most of us are aware of our religious rights in the general statement of the first amendment, but the fourteenth is even more critical in some ways. The fourteenth amendment states, "No state shall … deny to any person within its jurisdiction the equal protection of the laws."[6] That is more encompassing than most people realize. For starters, you cannot be asked your religion on a job application or in an interview. If you are asked such a thing, you do not have to answer, and the prospective employer cannot use that as a reason to not hire you. Along the same lines, you cannot be fired from a job because you are Wiccan. In fact, they do not have the right to even ask you

---

6 Fourteenth Amendment U.S. Const.

what your religion is once you are working there. If they do, you do not have to answer. If they fire you for being Wiccan, or refusing to answer a religion question, you have a court case, guaranteed by the fourteenth amendment.

Wicca being recognized by the US as a religion allows you to ask for our holidays off. Those holidays are even outlined nicely in the *Handbook for Chaplains*, if your employer needs evidence that February 2 is a Wiccan holiday. My favorite story about that is when I was still teaching as a college professor. Ostara was approaching.

I had no plans to take the day off because our rites take place mostly at night. I just happened to be in a meeting with our division's assistant chair. The topic came up. She knew I was Wiccan because I have been out of the Broom Closet for a long time. In that work environment religion, any religion, was just not a topic of conflict. She turned to me and asked if I wanted to take the spring equinox off because she also knew I was a High Priestess. I thanked her and said no. I laughed and added that for most pagan religions it is the day after the rite that we need to take off. It was a great moment of internal celebration for me of both my religion and my Constitution.

Before you ask for a day off for religious reasons, assess the climate. If you suspect there will be long-term consequences, make sure you are prepared to take on those consequences. As part of the asking, you might want to remember that the employer does have the right to have the holiday verified. Included in this particular topic is times of religious instruction. If you cannot work a particular shift because of religious instruction, then that is also covered under the fourteenth amendment, but you do have to supply some evidence that a class is taking place under a verified minister. The teacher, High Priestess, or High Priest should be able to verify that they are a licensed minister and the classes, whatever shape they take, are real. This makes a good argument for all of those folks out there who are teaching and leading circles and covens to go out and get licensed. It was one of the major reasons I did so.

Pitfalls and Warnings

While your employer can not fire you for being Wiccan, they can sure find something else. This is why it is so very important to assess whether or not to come out of the closet or even go back in. It can be very complicated to make a case of discrimination against the employer if they have let you go for failure to do your job, excessive absenteeism, bad conduct, or any of the multitude of things you can do wrong in the workplace. Some types of jobs are more sensitive than others. Folks who work with children might want to be very careful how they express their religious beliefs in the workplace. Where their kids are concerned, people get very involved, as they should.

Once you come out of the Broom Closet, there is nothing to stop coworkers, or other students, or neighbors, or anyone who has an issue with it, from acting in a discriminatory manner toward you. Only you can judge at what point that discrimination has reached the level that you take it to court. Most of the time it is the type of bigotry that is not really worthy of court time. However, if it's severely affecting your life at work, school, or other public arenas, or if someone comes onto your property and harms you or yours, call the police and a good lawyer.

If you are in trouble and feel the need for legal counsel, find someone that specializes in religious discrimination cases or call the local chapter of the ACLU (American Civil Liberties Union) and get some legal advice or aid. My suggestion is that you start with the ACLU because they have been around awhile and this is their bailiwick and they do good work. There is also the Lady Liberty League that is sponsored by Circle Sanctuary in Wisconsin.

Exercise
I Have a Right to Be Wiccan

You can express your power if you can avoid all of these issues. Sometimes a simple warding off your space at school or work will keep the troublemakers away from you. Do the exercise at home.

You will need: An object that gives you a sense of being protected. It should be relatively small and not eye-catching a blue candle, sage incense.

Cast a circle. Light the candle and the incense. Both of those correspond to Jupiter, the lawmaker. Invoke Jupiter. You can also invoke Hecate, the patron deity of witches.

Invest your object with the energy of the deity or deities you have invoked. While doing this visualize yourself protected from harm.

Open your circle. Take the object to wherever you need it. Place it near an entrance to your space, being careful that no one can trip over it.

Keep It Real

Overall, be a good citizen in our diverse world; many things need never be an issue if you do not make it one yourself. Going into the boss to ask for Wiccan holidays off is one thing. Walking around the workplace in full regalia despite any dress code at the job is quite another. Neighbors calling the police on you when you are quietly celebrating a sabbat in your backyard is very different from the neighbor calling the police because you have lit a dangerous bonfire in your backyard despite local ordinances that ban everyone from backyard burns.

Work with people instead of making it a challenge to which they feel compelled to respond. We are supposed to be working to make the world a better place, not a combat zone. Sometimes battles are unavoidable, and it is okay to fight when you are being discriminated against in an unfair manner, but do not be the problem yourself and throw down gauntlets to everyone around you.

Another way to make the world safer for pagans is to vote, especially at the state and local levels. Pay attention to what candidates are saying and respond accordingly. It is trendy and cool to appear to be apathetic to our political system, but we have the immense privilege of being able to voice our opinions, so voice those opinions. Vote! It does make a difference, especially at local levels where candidates can win or lose on a few votes. Believe it or not, what takes place at the local level is the beginning of what takes place at the national level. Voting is not a right, it is a privilege, one that many have died to obtain and keep for us. Use that privilege.

Things have changed a lot since I began my journey down the Wiccan pathway. When I first started it was nearly impossible to find books on the subject. You were lucky if you found practitioners of any type of magick and forget finding other witches. The advent of the internet changed the face of modern witchcraft and modern Wicca. In many places we barely stand out in the crowd. However, many witches are still hiding in the Broom Closet, usually for very good reasons. It is their decision when and how to emerge from that closet. The same rule applies here as it does to any other type of alternative lifestyle. Never "out" someone against their choice. It is your choice when and if to come out of the Broom Closet. Follow your heart to where you need to be. Just remember this. It is very easy to be a great and powerful witch if you are the only one in the closet. It is a much more difficult pathway once you are part of a group. There is no need to force the world to accept your choices, as long as you are joyous with the choice you have made.

CONCLUSION

I started down the witchcraft road over forty years ago. Finding other people who walked magickal and mystical pathways was beyond difficult. However, we did find each other, eventually. We shared our information and worked together. The internet has changed things in all ways. It is so easy now to connect with like-minded people. You can go online and access all types of information. I was classically trained, so I must offer this cautionary note. In the end, nothing works as well as reading the book for yourself. Nothing will assist your personal growth in the power of witchcraft more than working with other people. Things online can assist and be beneficial, but always take a minute to be sure that what you are reading and using has a basis of experience and truth behind it.

I've written a different type of book for witches. This book addresses how to use witchcraft to grow into your most powerful self. I was blessed that from the get-go, my compatriots and my teachers saw witchcraft as something that was so much more than casting a spell to achieve a specific end. Sometimes that is required, and I do not hesitate to cast a spell when needed. However, after all these years I also know that because I have walked the long walk of self-empowerment through using witchcraft, my spells are much more powerful and much more responsible. My spells work. Those spells work so well because I have reached into a greater part of my personal power. I reached that power because I used witchcraft to conquer my fears and let the magick work on me first and the world second. Your own power begins by conquering the fears inside you. Witchcraft can assist you in that process if you allow it to do so.

BIBLIOGRAPHY

Adler, Margot. *Drawing Down the Moon*. New York: Viking, 1979.

Aronson, Bonnie. "History of Shamanism" Accessed September 12, 2022. http://firstlightemp.com/history-of-shamanism .html.

Bolen, Jean Shinoda. *The Goddesses in Everywoman*. New York, New York: Harper & Row Publishers, 1985.

Bolen, Jean Shinoda. *The Gods in Everyman*. New York, New York: Harper & Row, Publishers, 1990.

Buckland, Raymond. *Complete Book of Witchcraft*. St. Paul, Minnesota: Llewellyn Publications, 1988.

Campanelli, Pauline. *Wheel of the Year: Living the Magical Life*. St. Paul, Minnesota: Llewellyn Publications, 1992.

Cunningham, Scott. *Wicca: A Guide for the Solitary Practitioner*. St. Paul, Minnesota: Llewellyn Publications, 1989.

Crowley, Aleister. *Magick in Theory and Practice*. New York: Dover Publications, Inc., 1976.

Crowley, Aleister. *Magick without Tears*. St. Paul, Minnesota: Llewellyn Publications, 1973.

Crowley, Aleister. *777 and Other Qabalistic Writings of Aleister Crowley*. York Beach, Maine: Simon Webster, Inc. 1996.

Dunham, Duwayne, director. *Halloweentown*. 1998; Disney Channel Original Movie, 1998. 84 minutes.

Farrar, Stewart, and Janet. *Eight Sabbats for Witches*. Custer, Washington: Phoenix Publishing Inc., 1981.

Hutton, Ronald. *The Triumph of the Moon*. New York: Oxford University Press, 2005.

Judith, Anodea. *Wheels of Life*. St. Paul, Minnesota: Llewellyn Publications, 1997.

K, Amber. *Covencraft*. St. Paul, Minnesota: Llewellyn Publications, 1998.

Myss, Caroline. *Why People Don't Heal and How They Can*. New York: Three Rivers Press, 1997.

Ravenwolf, Silver. *Solitary Witch*. St. Paul, Minnesota: Llewellyn Publications, 2004.

Ravenwolf, Silver. *To Ride a Silver Broomstick*. St. Paul, Minnesota: Llewellyn Publications, 1994.

Religious Requirements and Practices of Certain Selected Groups: A Handbook for Chaplains. Washington DC: Department of the Army, 1978.

Rowntree, Les, Martin Lewis, Marie Price, and William Wyckoff. *Diversity Amid Globalization: World Regions, Environments, Development*. Upper Saddle River, New Jersey: Pearson/Prentice Hall, 2009.

Starhawk. *The Spiral Dance*. San Francisco, California: Harper & Row Publishers, 1979.

NOTES

_____
_____
_____
_____
_____
_____
_____
_____
_____
_____
_____
_____
_____
_____
_____
_____
_____
_____

To Write to the Author

If you wish to contact the author or would like more information about this book, please write to the author in care of Llewellyn Worldwide Ltd. and we will forward your request. Both the author and the publisher appreciate hearing from you and learning of your enjoyment of this book and how it has helped you. Llewellyn Worldwide Ltd. cannot guarantee that every letter written to the author can be answered, but all will be forwarded. Please write to:

Linda Murphy
℅ Llewellyn Worldwide
2143 Wooddale Drive
Woodbury, MN 55125-2989

Please enclose a self-addressed stamped envelope for reply,
or $1.00 to cover costs. If outside the U.S.A., enclose
an international postal reply coupon.

Many of Llewellyn's authors have websites with additional information and resources. For more information, please visit our website at http://www.llewellyn.com.